# A WORKING CLASS WAR

*For everything there is a season,
and a time for every purpose under heaven:*

*a time to be born, and a time to die;*
*...*
*a time to kill, and a time to heal;*
*a time to break down, and a time to build up;*
*a time to weep, and a time to laugh;*
*a time to mourn, and a time to dance;*
*...*
*a time to keep silence, and a time to speak;*
*a time to love, and a time to hate;*
*a time for war, and a time for peace.*

*Ecclesiastes 3*

DEPTFORD FORUM PUBLISHING
110A New Cross Road
London SE14 5BA

First published 1995

© Deptford Forum Publishing Ltd

Interviews by Joy Vaughan and Rib Davis
Edited by Jess Steele
Design and Layout by Ed Fredenburgh
Cover by Lionel Openshaw
Printed by TU Printing Services, Newcastle

**Acknowledgements**

Among the Shinglers Hilda was the inspiration, while her daughter Joy Vaughan co-ordinated the family reminiscence and collected the memories. Among the Welches Richie played the main part while Rib Davis carried out the interviews.

Thanks to Stratford Community History Project, to Stratford City Challenge for having the vision to fund such work and to Geoff Bell whose idea it was. Thanks to Katya Phillips for transcribing, and to Karen Bray for her editing input.

Thanks to Michael Steele, Juliet Desailly and Christine Shearer for constructive comments and to Richard Walker for conceiving and organising the best launch voyage a book could hope for.

*Photographs* Imperial War Museum, front cover, 20, 41. Magnum, back cover. Topham Picturepoint, 2. BBC Hulton Picture Library, 12. Newham Local Studies Library, 24. All others supplied by the families

ISBN 1 898536 11 2

British Library Cataloguing in Publication Data
A catalogue record for this book is available from the British Library

# CONTENTS

Introduction     iv

**THE SHINGLER FAMILY**     1
**HARRY: doing what was right**     2
**JIM: round the markets**     8
**ELSIE: a working girl's war**     12
**LEN: running away**     20
**HILDA: city child, country child**     24
**RON AND TERRY: blanking out**     39

**THE WELCH FAMILY**     42
**ALF: clearing the bloody battlefields**     44
**GEORGE: eager for the sea**     53
**MARINA: sister of the seven gods**     60
**BILLY: under the Japs**     68
**ARTHUR AND KITTY: flat coins and cold baths**     81
**ROSIE: home and the hopfields**     90
**RICHIE: sixpence for Mum**     103

# INTRODUCTION

The Stratford Shinglers and the Deptford Welches have never met. They are different families with different backgrounds. What they have in common, as well as class and east London roots, is that within each family there is a wide range of experiences of the Second World War era. Here are conscientious objectors, prisoners of war, working women, evacuated children, front-line medics, sailors and little sisters left behind. Other family members, mentioned in passing, included deserters, tank recovery and those on the coastal gun posts. Inevitably there are some 'war functions' missing - air force, civil defence and the 'poor bloody infantry' being the most obvious. Happily, though perhaps untypically, not one member of either family was killed by enemy action.

It is strange that after six years of '50th anniversaries' and an unprecedented amount of 'revisiting' coverage from mass media to learned texts, there is still something to say about World War Two. The increasing recognition of oral history over the last 25 years has made this inevitable. Events within living memory have a potential for retelling from so many perspectives and the war is the last eventful era remembered by substantial numbers of people who were adults at the time. By the 100th anniversary, it will be too late for reminiscing.

The title arose out of the clear message from the interviews that the war, disruptive and disastrous as it was, did not fundamentally alter the class framework. Rather, that framework was adapted to fit the strange task of survival in a special era.

Young men from small communities were sent across the world to places they had never heard of with little explanation and less information. For them it was a time of unprecedented travel coupled with hardship and danger. Scattered around the globe, they moved on according to orders until taken by death, wounding, imprisonment or sudden peace. Others avoided soldiering but no-one could avoid the war.

Many urban children were evacuated to an idyllic but often hated countryside where they found the rules of life utterly different to their own. Others stayed in the blitzed city, picking hot shrapnel from school walls and putting the traditional skills of mischief-making and getting-by to practice in a context of no authority.

Women of all ages moved into the labour force or into previously unreachable aspects of it. Sometimes they evacuated with young children; more often they clung to home and the hope of survival even when the odds looked increasingly slim. Some moved house dozens of times and it began to seem as if 'Jerry' was following them down the street. They queued and haggled and made do, stretching each piece of food and clothing and their own precious energy close to breaking point.

While the thrust of this book describes an era of war, there is much incidental but valuable detail of the joys and tensions of working class family life. It offers a series of highly personal insights into the diversity of experience within just two families. Individuals, where they had a choice at all, made decisions based on their own perspective, their backgrounds and the opinions of other family members. Many of them still argue about it today but on both sides of the river, the families remain united - survivors of an era we must never forget.

# THE SHINGLERS

Henry Shingler Snr. was born in Spitalfields, East London in 1892. He married Rose Green of Bow in 1914 and they moved to Grace Road, Stratford. He was called up in the First World War and Rose went back to live with her family. They had nine children between 1915 and 1938. Two of the girls died as infants but the rest of the family survived and are still living today. Henry got a job on the railway which had a tied house on the Isle of Dogs. He lost the job in 1931 and became involved in the National Unemployed Workers' Movement. The family squashed into a single room at Henry's mother's house until they found a house in Hubbard Street, Stratford.

As the Shingler family grew they became renowned for noisy behaviour and rough living, but theirs was a large East End family in a harsh world and this was their reaction to it. Jim recalls: "We got thrown out of Hubbard Street. There were lots of complaints put in about us. The neighbours weren't much good, you see. There was a court case and Dad got his notice to quit from the private landlord." The Shinglers believed that as a family they were not respected in Stratford and this had a profound impact on their self-esteem. Elsie Shingler felt this particularly acutely. She made friends outside the Stratford area "because a lot of people down there believed I was a Shingler. But I'm not, I always looked nice and smart and different."

Despite this ambivalence, the Shinglers stuck together through much of the war. These stories show them as diverse characters coming to terms with family needs, loyalties and disappointments through the heartaches of evacuation and the innumerable uncertainties of war.

## The Shingler family

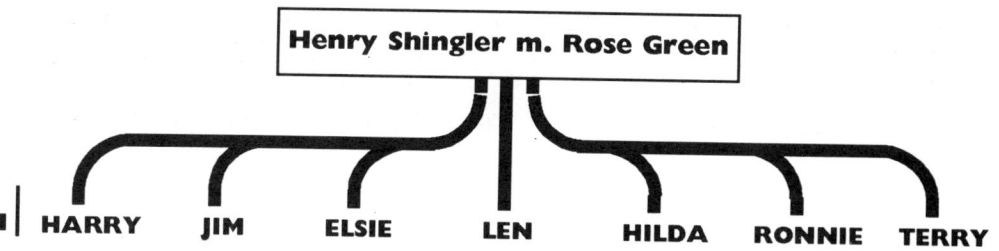

# HARRY

## doing what was right

Harry Shingler was born in 1915 in Bromley-by-Bow. The family lived in Millwall during his childhood and moved to Stratford around 1937.

Faced with the huge unemployment of the 1930s and unable to find regular work, Harry became a socialist at the age of 16. He went to socialist meetings at Conway Hall, and to the big rallies at Hyde Park. "I listened to them and they seemed very logical, conditions being what they were. I still think their analysis is correct of the system itself, of capitalism. But bringing about socialism, that's another matter, that's where they fall down."

Harry's politics and his personal observations gave him an understanding of the causes of the war beyond the propaganda put out by governments.

Given his opinions on the underlying purpose of war and its futility for the working classes, he refused to enroll and was imprisoned as a conscientious objector.

I got interested in politics because I couldn't get a regular job in the 1930s. The only one I ever had was in the Post Office long after the war, from 1961 until 1975. Before that it was all odd jobs – three months here, three months there. I worked hard to try and keep my job but it didn't matter. They would come in and say, "You, you, and you are finished tonight". It happened time and time again.

One time they sent me and another bloke to Brentwood to pick up a load of bricks all covered with ice. I was frozen, but when I was finished I got the sack. Another time I was digging a trench in frozen ground. They've got a digger now, but then it was a pickaxe and a shovel. Then I had another at Ford's unloading timber – two bob an hour – you had to go up and down, up and down.

**Becoming political**

I got my inspiration from the Socialist Party of Great Britain, founded in 1904. It was and is the real Marxist party. I listened to them, they were right about the war and society. They put the real programme of Marxism forward; other parties who said they were socialist were confused about it. Marxism is the true economics, not capitalism. All capitalists want is to make as much money as they can, profit before life. Money is dominant, life is nothing. It's chaos all the way. I thought people would do something about it; I think they'll have to before long. It's not a planned economy, it's all in the interest of the people running it.

The Labour Party's not socialist; they're not even good reformists. When they get in they take notice of the people with money, so they can't do anything. If the people with money say no reform that means no reforms because they cost money and it would have to come out of their profits, so they're against it. So the Labour party can't even be good reformists, let alone anything else.

As for the Communist Party, that wasn't communist. What you had in Russia at that time was state capitalism. The core of the Russian revolution was Peace, Land, Bread. That was what the revolution was fought for and after, when Lenin tried to introduce communism, he couldn't because people didn't understand what it was about. Also, it can't work in one country. It has to work in several countries. Everything is international and if it isn't it doesn't work.

When the Soviet Union started getting advanced, from 1930 onwards, getting a big army and building factories, amassing goods, the capitalists saw this as a danger to their markets, and the army as a threat to them. But it wasn't communism, it was state capitalism which threatened their market, threatened their profit. Russian goods were making profits. So it wasn't communism because communism isn't about making profits, it's about common ownership. Even so it was a rival to Britain and America. Their big aim was to stop it.

**Harry's version of the war**

My version of the war. The war started because Germany was a threat to the British Empire. Hitler was doing the dirty work for the German capitalists. They wanted the British Empire and they wanted their own empire back in North Africa which they had lost in the First World War.

All wars are fought over trade. If someone's standing in their way, they use force. They go to war to stop the country going under. They only get on through war. Wars make plenty of work. It's the only way they can make work in this society, having wars every now and again. People are killed by arms their own side sells to the so-called enemy. Those who sell arms don't care what happens as long as they get the profit. They don't refuse any customer – you got the money, you're in. Before the war America was supplying arms to Germany.

I was working in 1938 for a firm called Free Trade Wharf in Wapping. Every morning I used to go to work and see Nazi boats load up with old iron. Nazi flags flying in the back of the boat. The firm selling the iron was called Cohen 600. They was selling it to

Germany. What was it being used for? Maybe it was turned into bombs to be dropped on this country in the war. I saw it with my own eyes. See what sort of hypocrites they are? I took notice of that. God knows how much money they got. As long as they got the money they'd sell to anybody. That's capitalism.

Before the war Germany's building up. They were going to attack Russia because it had a different system and they could see if Russia got industrialised they'd be supplying the world and the Germans wouldn't be able to sell their goods. Germany was built up, but who built it up? In 1919 it was a bankrupt country, wasn't worth a penny. I think it was this country and America built it up to smash Russia, because Russia was talking about capitalism this and capitalism that and the capitalists here didn't like it. So Germany was built up to attack Russia, but when they got strong enough they didn't do that, they went through Poland. You also had fighting in the Middle East where the British Empire was. The plan was to get Germany and Russia to annihilate each other; then they would come and dictate all the terms. But it was a plan that went wrong.

On September 3rd Chamberlain was waiting for an answer. It never came. "I must tell you now", he said, "we have had no answer from Germany and this country and Germany are at war." Had Germany attacked Russia right away it would have been a different story.

Germany wanted their empire back and they were going to leave Russia till last. That was why they signed the Hitler-Stalin pact, to get oil from Russia to fight in the Middle East. I don't understand why Russia signed that pact, it was a stab in the back.

In 1933 when Hitler got to power, Germany had a big Communist Party. What they done to stop the communists getting into power, they set fire to the Reichstag – their own parliament – and said the communists done it, but they done it themselves. That made Hitler's vote go up in leaps and bounds because people will believe anything.

During that time Churchill, who was always against communism, said "If I was a German living in Germany I would welcome Adolph Hitler wholeheartedly." That was because he was against communism. Of course he changed his tune when there was a war on. He didn't mind fascism because it was against communism. They aren't as against fascism as they make out, but they certainly don't want socialism. They would sooner have fascism than communism. Fascism is capitalism in its most brutal form. One thing about the people in this country is that they haven't supported fascism. It's up to the people. If the people support it like they did in Germany, you can't do nothing about it.

I heard one man say at the grocer's shop, If it wasn't for Churchill we wouldn't have won the war, he gave the lead. But if that's the case, the time the next war comes along all they have to do is put some of his old speeches on.

### The workers' country?

I had a job filling sand bags then. Sunday morning, September 3rd, Chamberlain said "Now this country is at war with Germany". Remember the words, remember the speech.

The Communist Party here were shouting in the streets, "We've got to stop Hitler, let's have a second front now". But I thought it was a capitalist war, it was nothing to do with the workers. And I remembered that in 1933 Churchill had said he admired Hitler.

**I'm not clever. I just say what I think. The words are flowing.**

The people were out of work. They would join the army to get work, to do something different. The majority of people were caught up in it, they never really thought about it. They thought they would fight for their country like their fathers did in the First World War. Those who fought in the Second World War thought they were fighting for their country and that the country belonged to them. But the only time the country could belong to them is when it's commonly owned by everyone and it's not, its owned by developers and millionaires. But they went to war because they believed it was their country. You tell me what their country is, where is it? I want to know where mine is. When they come out of the First World War they was begging in the streets. Where was their country?

What have the workers got? They've got nothing. We have to do something for us, all of us, not the capitalists. Some of these people who sent you off to war, they never done a stroke of work in their lives. It's not their brain that makes the money, it's the people who do the work that makes the money. It's the workers who make the profits for the capitalists.

I remember before the Second World War people used to say "I ain't going to go to war no more" but they did. They got good propaganda and they went. "Never again", they said after the First World War, but they went.

The government don't want you to think about wages or longer holidays, because that's got to be paid for out of their profits. So they fool you with propaganda. They want to brutalise your mind so you don't think about anything that matters. The government's not going to say what the war's really about. Instead they say "You have to fight for your country, or else Hitler will be here. He'll be coming over tonight on his plane."

The workers didn't profit from the Second World War. They profit from no wars. The rulers love the dead because the dead don't cost nothing. Never mind about the living, the dead don't cost nothing so they go on about the dead. Why do they show all these war films on the television? To keep the people war-minded. If people were non-violent it would be no bloody good to them in case they need them to go to war again.

Henry Ford idolised Hitler. It was like the Falklands war. They weren't worried about what sort of regime they had in Argentina. They fought over the Falklands, what one had and the other wanted. During the war they went on about all these people missing in Argentina. Why didn't Thatcher say all that before? It was all just propaganda. They weren't worried about the system, only when it became a threat to them.

Let me tell you about a great man, Tony Turner. He died two years ago. At a political meeting he said "Do you people want to take part in a war?" This was a trick question, a question you got no answer to. How could you answer that, the war was on. He was so good, you couldn't get one over on him. It was not the Communist Party, nothing to do with them.

### Going to prison

I thought of number one because of the life I had before the war. I thought to myself, I ain't putting my life on the line for that. What gave me the idea also was knowing about the First World War, young boys being machine-gunned. All that led up to my ideas, the First World War and the 1930s and all that. I knew this society had something wrong with it.

I was put in jail for my views. They came round for me and took me down Stratford police court. I said to my mother "I got to go to court, for what I've done". I said "Ma, I'll be back", but I never came back. They took me straight down there, put me right away. They put you in a big motor, black maria, I couldn't see nothing. They give you all the details: "if you want to survive in prison you have to..." — all this sort of thing. They all know your case. They said to me "turn all your pockets out on the table: money and whatever". You had to say sir this and sir that. Then you had to get a uniform, get the stuff, put it on. They sent a parson in.
"Are you going through with this?"
"Certainly I am."

"Are you a Christian?"

It was Wormwood Scrubs first and then they put us in Wandsworth. I was there for six or seven months.

My friend Ted Cox was a CO. I met him about 1934. He lived in Bromley-by-Bow in a block of flats. He shared my political views but he argued his case and he got off. He had a good case. He knew what the war was about and they knew he was right. You got to show them you know what it's all about. They ain't going to tell you. He beat them at the tribunal and he got off. He beat them with words, because they knew he knew what the war was about. They were frightened what he'd tell others in there.

You want to know what it was like? They kept me locked up 17 hours a day, in the freezing cold winter of 1940. The worst winter I ever had, I wouldn't be able to do it now. A little cell, no bed, no sheets, no bath. Sit in there for 17 hours. The time they did let me out I had to go on parade, little thin coat, ice on the bloody roof. I'd be marching around this square with all kinds of people, murderers and all sorts. After you did your walking round they shut you up and then after that you sewed mail bags. I didn't put mine out. It was too bloody cold, I used them to keep myself warm. Before they took you to the cell if you had good behaviour you would all sit round a table and talk and have all your food together. You got your food in a tin, your dinner in a tin. But 17 hours a day I was shut up there, bloody cold it was, like the Tower of London.

I came out of prison because they had a job for me. They asked me what work I would like to do. So I told them I would do demolition work. They realised it was a waste of time keeping you in there when there was work to be done outside. Some there wouldn't do any work; the Peace Pledge Union. They wouldn't do anything for the war, no work at all they said. But I was glad to get out of there, to take anything. They were happy to throw me out. So I worked for this firm Charles Griffiths, doing all this demolition.

I felt funny when I came out. As I came out the big doors banged behind me. Prison officers, all young blokes, they say what they like to the COs. I heard them outside talking, grinding other people down.

But what I did was right. These people who took part in the war didn't know what it was about. If people didn't take part in war there would be no war at all – just like that. But for everyone that didn't go there would be 20 that would. There wasn't many that didn't go but if there was, there wouldn't have been any bloody war, would there? If people said "We've got enough to put up with as it is, we don't want no capitalist wars", there wouldn't be any. And what do these people get out of it? Those people who went to Dunkirk to commemorate that, they wouldn't even pay their fare over there.

## The war comes to Harry

I was in Charge Square when they dropped a bomb on the labour exchange. As I got to the back entrance all the stuff come down, girders, stones, masonry. I just managed to get in the door. A brick hit me in the arm, my arm was opened up. I went and got inside there. All the candles had gone and I had to sit all night long, me arm in a sling. Now if I'd have got in quicker I would have been smashed. Girders, curb stones all ended up in that area. It all fell round where I was running, running for all I was worth. Just got indoors in time.

HILDA: *He had a tin of crab inside his sling what he'd pinched, picked up off the pavement, so me, him and mum had a crab sandwich and she said 'Oh, you shouldn't do that, they could shoot you'.*

A flying bomb came over. It came down the street and fell at Temple Mill. I was walking past the Grove Picture House in Stratford with Ted Cox. Christ Almighty, that made us jump out of our skin as it came over. I said to Ted Cox, "Quick, into that doorway" and I pushed him. In another minute a big lump of shrapnel come through the glass room. If he'd been standing there one minute more he'd be gone. I don't know what made me give him a push, I saved his life. You got used to the flying bombs. You'd see it and say "Oh, bugger it" and you'd keep waiting. I went in one day to the shop at Angel Lane and this bomb dropped and blew the door off and it banged right up against me as it dropped.

## Sheltering

There were always the lights shining up in the sky. Any minute I thought something would happen, All the ammunition trucks there, ready to go away. The German planes, a couple of bombs.

We used to go under Stratford to shelter in the underground station. There was a tunnel and it wasn't finished so they made it into a shelter because when the war started they couldn't carry on with it. It was terrible down there. People had their beds down there and there was no sanitation or nothing. People came up to us, me and Ted Cox, and asked if we had a bunk down there. He'd given his up to a woman. We just stopped down there until the raid had abated a bit. So I went home to the shelter in the garden. In the finish I used to go home and go to bed. I was so fed up with it, I just wanted to go to sleep. All your clothes were sweaty oh, for a couple of years or more, day after day after day.

I don't know how we got through it. Rockets, no warning at all. All you see at night is the sky then they are going to drop. During the Second World War you were just waiting and waiting for the sirens to go. Then when it did you had to try and get to a shelter. Then there was the rockets and you didn't have time to get a warning. All you saw was a big flash and you knew it was going to drop. People still went about their business. After a while people didn't think about the danger. They got so complacent, so used to it. Well, you couldn't do anything about it, could you? The buses were still running, people were about in the streets. You never knew when anything was going to happen – no warning. Big bloody things would come down all of a sudden.

## Entertainment

I was unemployed for a while but, mind you, there was always somewhere to go; the music hall, the Lyons cafe, the cinema. There was always cinema to go to – sixpence for a four hour programme. It was lovely, but sometimes people would be making a nuisance. They'd be behind you talking and all that and you couldn't listen. But really I preferred that more than the telly. The telly's like looking into a bloody tomb. With the cinema you had the big screen. If you went in the afternoon there would be nobody in. It was quiet then, lovely it was. But at night time they would all go in after work and they'd talk. I've seen a lit fag thrown over the top of the balcony. You still got vandalism then, though it's on a larger scale now.

## Changing Times

You always met someone in the street; now, you don't see nobody. When I went around looking for work in them days I used to run into people I knew all the time.

There were lots of shops and stalls in Stratford. People were satisfied then if they had a shop or a stall. As long as they took their rent they were satisfied, as long as they had enough to carry on. Now people want more and more. Lots of people didn't have the money to pay the shopkeeper at the time, so he wrote what they bought down in a book and they paid him at the end of the week. They made a living enough to keep the shop going. There was lots of shops then, no big supermarkets like now.

The bread was good then, tuppence ha'penny a loaf of bread, all full of dough. Now they don't put flour in it. The days of value are gone, you got good value then. Now they charge you more and it ain't so good.

# JIM round the markets

Jim was called up despite his poor eyesight. He trained at Clacton-on-Sea and was assigned to the Pioneer Corps, an auxiliary army unit for men with disabilities.

He worked on army salvage at Dulwich and then at Crystal Palace. He enjoyed the work until day he broke his glasses and was sent to get a new pair. When the doctor tested his eyes it was discovered that he was blind in one eye and the cataracts in the other meant he could only see with glasses.

He was discharged from the Pioneer Corps and made his way back to Stratford.

With help and encouragement from his father he hired a barrow and board and spent the war selling kettles and other scarce household goods around the markets of East London.

*Rathbone Street market*

At the start of the war I was called up to have a medical to go in the army. I thought I'd got away with it with my bad eyes so I came home happy. Anyway a policeman come in Mum's shop in Angel Lane and said "I want you to report. You're supposed to be in the army and they want you." "Not to my knowledge", I said. I hadn't heard anything and I thought I was out of it. But he said "According to my confirmation, you've got to report to Clacton-on-Sea, the Butlins Holiday Camp".

## To Butlins under orders

I got my papers and I went to Clacton-on-Sea. No holiday-makers there, only the army. The army took over all the holiday camps, drilling, marching, *one two, one two, back two*, cos there was just the right space for that. When I got there I was so fed up I felt like crying. I had no dinner when I got there, didn't fancy it. Homesick, wasn't I? Anyway I got settled in. There were chalets for sleeping in. The army had taken over all the facilities of the holiday camp.

I was in the Pioneer Corps. All disabled people went in that and I had bad eyes. The others, they had all their limbs but was disabled in some other way. They showed you things in the Pioneer Corps, in case you had to meet the enemy – how to use a rifle and all the drills and marching, about gases, everything. If there was an emergency or a bomb dropped somewhere and there's all the wreckage and debris laying about, you had to go and clear it all up.

## Salvage work

Eventually we got our orders to shift. They had taken over all these big houses in Beckenham in Kent. Probably the people who owned these properties must have gone abroad, back to their families perhaps. We still went out on different jobs clearing up for the army. I was reporting for duty and all of a sudden I got me orders. I gotta go and work on army salvage. I had to report to Dulwich at the barracks there. In the corner of the drill ground you had a corporal. He had a little hut filled with bottles and cardboard and paper. He was collecting army salvage and I had to report to him.

Then they discovered that hut was too small for him to carry on in that facility. So they sent him to a big depot at Crystal Palace. They took the railway booking hall over as a salvage dump. I went with him. The crack regiments, like the Guards and the Fusiliers, used to bring all their stuff: bottles, cardboard, newspapers and what have you, all to help in the war effort. I suppose they brought the bottles out of the officers' mess. Then they put Jock in charge and when he set up the booking hall for the army salvage he got himself an office, a desk, a paper machine. All the stuff we collected was sorted out and parceled up. The packets would be baled up and taken away by lorry to different parts of the country to help in the war effort. I was happy in that army salvage. I can't remember plain what I got a week. It wasn't a lot but being disabled they let you off the leash a bit.

We had a nice little mess room with a gas stove. The Royal Army Ordnance Corps were across the way. They had old boys working for them, civilians. They was creosoting big tarpaulin sheets and doing all kinds of odd jobs in the army. That Crystal Palace grounds was where they tested the lorries. They would repair them and run them all round the grounds and look at the engines when they were going round to see if they was alright. It was a big depot for the army.

One day the sergeant came by a lovely big statue of a naked woman. He found it in the hallway of the salvage depot which was in the booking hall of the station. It probably came from the old Crystal Palace before the fire of 1936. He said "I'll take this back and give the boys a treat" but he opened the back of the truck and it fell out and broke up into pieces.

I was quite happy. I used to come home at weekends sometimes. On my weekend I used to go in the pub with me dad, in the Lion. I quite enjoyed the band in the Lion and a nice drink. One time I was coming back off a leave and I was forced to go down a big under-ground shelter down Whitechapel way. While I was in this shelter all the people kept coming in crying and sobbing. Someone must have got killed outside the shelter.

## Disaster

Anyway I broke me glasses on salvage, didn't I? I couldn't see, and yet I was supposed to have been a chap to go against a German. I had the rifle drill and all that goes with it to face the enemy. Because if the Pioneers went abroad to help with the regular soldiers they might have to defend themselves. But I broke me glasses and I had to report to the army medical. So then he found I was blind in one eye and the eye I could see out of was no good without the glass. Cataract in this right eye, without the glass I can't see on it, and the other eye was blind. So he gives me a good eye test and he says "Sit down on the stall a minute will you. I'll take a look at ya". But instead of me sitting down on the stall, I sat on the bleeding floor. Couldn't see it at all and I just went arse over head.

Anyway, I goes back, reports for duty, carries on with me work. All of a sudden the corporal comes out and says "Jim, you're not allowed on the road. You're not allowed out nowhere. You're getting an army discharge." He said "I'll keep you here for a little while and then I'll get somebody to escort you to the station to see you're alright." Army discharge.

I had been so happy, you know, going backwards and forwards in the army depot. I had to report to a depot in Luton to get my discharge and the poor men was standing down there, half asleep and half dead they were, in their bleeding dirty old overalls, half dead with work. I made me way towards London and as I was struggling through the main station coming home there was all these red caps, army police. I felt so happy thinking of them. They stopped and I marched through them to come home.

In the Pioneers I wore a uniform same as a soldier and I had a rifle. In an emergency, like an invasion, we would have been part of the army. But then me glasses would have fallen off and they would have killed me. What chance would I have had? Picture me going against the Germans and me glasses fall off. That's why they wouldn't have me.

## A complete change

Things were different. I was no good to nobody. I didn't get called in by the labour, I was fit for nothing. Nobody bothered with me. I was so depressed. I got stick from people having these cataracts but I just ignored them. Having these cataracts in the eyes, it makes you rather backwards all your life.

When I come back Dad come up to me and I told him all me business. He kinda felt sorry for me, the old man, coming out of the army half bleeding blind. He said to me "Jim, you got any money?" I said "Yeah, I got a few bob". "Right-o, I'll tell you what to do. Come with me. We'll go down to the tinware factory. We'll buy some tin stuff and sell it down the market. I think you'll like that. You'll be alright".

So we got a barrow and board. We used to hire it from Parrott's. We went all round the markets and I quite enjoyed that. The one I liked best and worked the most was Homerton market in Hackney. It had shops and stalls there. In the end they gave me a licensed pitch, a regular one. I also did Chris Street market in Poplar, Rathbone Street in Bow, Queen's Road in Upton Park, Woolwich market, all over. Selling all this household stuff. That was about 1942 or 1943. It was so scarce people thought it come out of the sky. We made a good living cos nobody was making household commodities, only Fingelsteins. We'd go down there, buy a load of kettles and take them down the market. We had seven pound each one week.

If the warning went in the daytime and we were in the market, there usually wasn't anything happening and it was all over in about five minutes. They had the fighters going up. They were a protection. The warning used to go and about half an hour later it would be the all-clear. We had a two year lull during the war when nothing happened. You wouldn't think there was a war on. No enemy there. That's when I think I done me most trade round the markets.

## Fire-watching

Later when the bombs were dropping I done a bit of fire-watching. I wanted to do something to help a bit in the war. It was voluntary like the neighbourhood watch would be now; they asked for volunteers. The offices were in Kaylee's shop, a suit shop opposite where we lived in Angel Lane, run by a Jew man. You went along to the shop and said "I'm volunteering to do a bit of fire-watching". So say an incendiary dropped, you'd alert somebody in case of emergency. It wasn't a bomb as such. When it dropped it went round and round like a bleedin' top in the road and went up in flames.

They'd have a load of men and women sitting watching in a room with binoculars and looking around for fires what nobody knew they was having because there was no bang. You had a bucket with water and a stirrup pump and if you saw one you had to get there quickly. It was terrible that all these firemen got killed putting out the fires when the bombs were dropping.

To do firewatching, you went to the shop and waited for Mr Caine. He was in charge and the leader but he was an old man. He never done nothing else. You'd stay there. Our old man loved it. He would take some drinks over and cards.
*How did you get the bucket to the fire?*
HILDA: *In every shop you went in there was a red bucket that said FIRE.*

Well, as it happens, I never got to that stage of putting any fires out. I never had occasion to use it. What I did was called the alarm.

## Shelter or bed?

I only went down the shelter in the yard once and I went down the tunnel once. You could hear the bombs coming over all night long, droning. But mostly I stayed in bed, took a bleeding chance.

HILDA: *They never went in the shelter because they were men and they thought it was stupid and silly.*

Yeah, I just looked at it and went to bed and took a chance.

What with the war being on and everybody thinking it could have been their bleeding lot and the invasion about to happen, we had to make our own happiness. We was all quite happy. Used to go in the pub every night, in the Lion. Elsie's husband, Harold, was in there playing in the band. We could mix in there. Piano and drums and people singing 'That Lovely Weekend' and 'Coming in on a Wing and a Prayer'. But while all that was going on, there was bombs dropping all around but we just stayed in the pub.

I was very lucky. I was never on the scene after a bomb dropped. I never see any devastation, never see anybody lying in the road or anything, or lying half dead. I lived in Stratford and furthest I went out was Hackney. I never worried or got frightened. I just took it as it come.

# ELSIE

## a working girl's war

Elsie Shingler was born in 1922 in Bromley-by-Bow. She was living in Waddington Street, Leyton, when the war broke out. She remembers the sound of the sirens and people running around shouting "the war's on!". "I went all hysterical because I didn't understand and Jim whacked me round the face."

As well as looking after her young brothers before they were evacuated, Elsie worked throughout the war, starting at a sausage canning factory in Stratford. She avoided the munitions factories because the work was "too tedious".

She met her husband in Woolwich while he was waiting for a discharge having been wounded abroad. They moved to his sister's house in Yorkshire where they married. In 1944 Elsie and Harold returned to Stratford where Elsie did her best to set up home despite the devastation of the city and the ongoing insecurity of life in a war zone.

Everyone was talking about getting gas masks. My brother Terry was a little baby and the old man went to get one but they wouldn't let him have it so he nicked one. I think he was one of the first people in Stratford to get nicked when the war started. When they come and took him away we was all crying. I'm not sure but I think he got about six weeks in prison, just for taking the gas mask for the baby.

The family moved into Angel Lane in the winter of 1940. Then it all went quiet for a while. The war was quiet for about a couple of years and then it started getting real bad. I remember the sirens going during the day. Angel Lane was the market and everyone was running away, all the stalls were left.

Then people started going down shelters, the ones they made in their gardens. When it got real bad they went down the tubes. I wouldn't go down them. I didn't like that.

## Family misfortunes

When Mum was pregnant with Terry she used to go to bed for the afternoon. The funny part was that I never knew how to cook. There were lots of things I didn't know how to do. The old man was always out on the beer so he didn't help out. He only gave me two bob a day to get food. I was 16 then and I just had to get on with looking after everything.

When the war started Ronnie was four and Terry was two. Before the war I used to look after Ronnie a lot. As a matter of fact I really brought him up until he was evacuated. I used to take him to the pictures a lot when he was a baby to see cowboy pictures and comedies. I remember one day at the Playhouse in Chant Square, the raids were on and we were the only two in there. They turfed us out, said it wasn't worth showing the film. We didn't get our money back either.

Terry had his legs broken by rickets. He had this plaster on his legs, thick stuff. They didn't keep him in hospital, he came home. The poor little sod was wrapped like a parcel all the way up. Being a baby, he was miserable. He was screaming and screaming in pain. Sometimes we used to go to the shelter in Great Eastern Road with Mum and cos he used to keep crying she'd say "I can't stand this, I'm going now". She walked out, carrying him, and when we were out the old man came over. He was dead drunk. Terry was screaming and my dad got a hammer and knocked all the plaster off his legs.

Terry went away to Devon about 1941. Mum took him and left him there with these people. I said to her "What you want to do a thing like that for? He's only a baby?" She said "Oh well, it's best, with everything on and all that". So then she didn't have any kids to look after. She used to go to the pictures and she used to go shopping a bit but she was never much of a one for shopping. She used to go round the little grocer's shop called the Jubilee Shop in Waddington Street.

When she got that shop in Angel Lane during the war all the people were buying her furniture. Then utility furniture came out. She just used to sell a few bits and pieces, anything she could get hold of. She had an old-fashioned tea chest under the table and that used to be full up of money.

*Did you pay 'keep' to your mum and dad?*

Paid keep sometimes. If I wasn't there I'd say "Well, I ain't had that". I used to go round to mates a lot and I had a lot of food there.

## Getting out and away

I started going out with mates. We used to go out to Stratford a lot, and to Woolwich. We used to have a good time over there and meet soldiers and have a laugh and all that. This mate of mine at work asked if I wanted to go out one night. I wasn't sure but she said, "Oh come on, get yourself all dolled up". In them days I had what you called a picture hat, like a round page-boy's hat, so I put that on and dolled myself up. We went over to Woolwich and had a lovely time. We went into a pub and had a drink. There was entertainment like pianos and everyone was nice and friendly and laughing. We met some more people and went to a dance place called the Catholic Club.

---

"Women never smoked hardly at all till war started. They started when the war came because they tried to be like men, doing all the men's jobs. They started getting all independent. They wasn't housewives anymore, they were going out to work."

---

We still went to musicals. I used to like chorus girls and comedians. We went out to the pictures two or three times a week. I saw the Wizard of Oz during the war. I liked Randolph Scott and John Wayne.

You could get a sixpenny ticket from six o'clock to twelve o'clock at night to go where you liked. You bought it from the bus conductor. We used to go over to Woolwich, backwards and forwards on the bus. We used to have larks with the bus drivers. The ferry was running in the war as well.

My mates weren't from Stratford. I used to go further afield because a lot of people down there, they all believed I was a Shingler. The Shinglers lived all wrong, they didn't care and they were all scruffy. But I always looked nice and smart and different, you know what I mean? I had a rotten old life in a way and I was glad to get out and get away.

### Make-do fashion

When I went out I'd wear whatever was the fashion, but a lot of them we couldn't get. Before the war I dyed my hair a bit with peroxide. My hair was like a golden colour. When it started to grow out, all the roots were going black, but we couldn't get peroxide so it went dark again. You couldn't buy hair curlers but one of the girls at work told me to buy pipe cleaners and double them in half. Then another fashion came out on war work. We used to cut the top off an old stocking and put it round our hair like a turban. In summertime a little beret hat on the side of your head was fashionable.

Since we couldn't get stockings we used to put on leg make-up. You went to the chemist to get it. One Saturday my mates and me were going out to a dance. All the shops used to shut at five o'clock on Saturday. My mate ain't got any make-up for her legs so I told her to buy some cocoa, cos it was dark, and put it on her legs so it looked like a tan. We were in a dance hall and the bleeding cocoa melted on her legs! We were trying to make our legs brown coloured. I never shaved my legs, though. That's one thing I never done. I don't know if others did.

Sometimes you'd wear earrings. I never had me ears done, I used to wear clips. We'd have a hat pulled over one ear and just wear one earring. I used to have court shoes with plain high heels and they were always smart. The elders wore a shoe that laced up the middle.

You used to buy a tube of lipstick in Woolworths for sixpence. They still sold it during the war, not so frequent but you could get it. You could buy everything in Woolworths. They sold bracelets, necklaces and rings. In those days girls used to wear artificial flowers on their coats or dresses and they sold those. They also sold torches, shampoo and soap. Woolworths never sold anything over sixpence. It was a threepenny and six-penny place and it was all put out with big lights.

Marks and Spencers had nothing costing over five shillings. They sold clothes. You could get a lovely blouse for two shillings and sixpence. For five shillings you could get a wrist watch.

There was one stall down Angel Lane called the Hole in the Wall that sold all different stockings. They had patterned ones and the ones with the line up the back. We used to enjoy the shopping. After my friend and I had got all our bits we used to go to my house and have a bit of tea and then we'd get ready and go out.

**Pubs and romance**

The beer was better then. I used to like a bottle of brown ale. I'd mostly go up to the bar in a pub but in them days women didn't do it so much, the men did. But when we went out with mates we'd all go up together.

*Did you get off with blokes in pubs?*

Oh, blow me yeah, I should say so! They walked you home and that. Hilda met a soldier in Devon and she told him all about me and he sent me chocs. I don't know what his name was, I never saw him. He wanted to get right friendly. People in them days couldn't take a chance so much because they didn't know when they would go away or whether they were going to get killed or not. Some of them might be married men and you never knew. They were all in the army and a lot of them might know they were going away but were not allowed to say. So you took a chance on who you went with. Some of them used to come from Manchester and all them places. Unless you get right together, you couldn't come and visit every day from there could you?

When all the Americans started coming over, I went with one. They would give the girls nylons and chewing gum. Those who were single then had the time of their life. And, my God I tell you, the Americans had more money than an English soldier. I think the English got 21 shillings a week and if he wanted to he gave his mum so much of that a week. Jim never did with my mum. She said "that tight git".

I also went with an Australian up where the Serpentine is in Hyde Park. We went out on the rowing boats. It was bloody good. A great big bloke, about six foot, in a suit. I went out with a Canadian for a while but when they went home you didn't really bother to keep in touch. There was one bloke from Manchester that I was in love with and he kept writing to me. Sometimes the soldiers got posted but they didn't know when they were going. It was a secret. He got called away and I didn't know but he sent another soldier with a message for me. I was so fed up I didn't know what to do with myself. I had such a rotten home life, so I just started going out and that was how I met my husband. Mum told me she was still getting the letters while I was up in Yorkshire, but when I got married she tore them up.

You'd sometimes go with one and you didn't like him, then you wouldn't go with him. Then you'd go across on the ferry and tell them to wait over the other side and all that lark. On Saturday afternoons we'd go to the shops and have our photos taken, sometimes with them, sometimes on our own. I had a photo taken when they were doing the fire watchers, all with our trousers on. They used to call them slacks. I had a gabardine coat as well.

**Shelters**

Everywhere you went there was a notice up saying SHELTER. We had air raid shelters in Stratford where everyone used to go. People would come round selling tea and playing the accordion. Others used to go in the Woolworths in Stratford for shelter. There was big girders in this place. My friend Phil and his mate went in there. His mate said "I don't half feel hungry" so he went to get something but Phil stayed there. As the boy left, the place got a direct hit and one of the girders fell on his back. He died about five minutes after. Loads of people got killed.

When you heard the sirens go, sometimes the raid lasted about an hour. So you just made sure you went into a shelter. They had shelters locally, stone ones. Inside they were just concrete and uncomfortable. I never liked sleeping or staying down the shelters because I couldn't stand the atmosphere down there. All the people were crowded together and breathing over you and there was no privacy. It smelt really musty as well.

If we heard an air raid while we were in Woolwich I'd stay in a big public shelter. You'd all be down there, singing and laughing. They had lights down there but there was all rubbish, people eating and sleeping there in the rubbish. People had bunks and blankets but we didn't do all that. We just sat and talked. You used to make your own amusement. A geezer had a mouth organ and fags there and a drink. Like a little orgy! Yeah, we had some good times as well as bad times.

People just carried on as normal during the raids. They went to work and everything. There were special shelters at work, places that you could go and when the raid finished you'd go back to work. They still paid you for that time you weren't working.

## Elsie's accident

I had the accident in 1941. There was this girl I knew at school and she joined the ATS. When she come home I hadn't seen her for ages and she suggested we go to the Green Man in Leytonstone for a night out. I was dubious at first but we went. When we got in the pub I went down to the toilets. In them days you had gaslight globes and it wasn't on. I remember going down the stairs, going outside, and then I don't remember no more. I was unconscious for three days and in hospital for six weeks on the danger list. I had permanent damage. I cracked all my ear bones and I was never the same with headaches. I got compensation of £75. That was a lot then.
*Did you just go and spend it all?*

No, not really, cos the old man took a lot of it.

## Marriage

After the accident I started going out again and met another fella who lived in Stratford and I was going with him. Then I met my Harold at Woolwich and went with him. He was in the army, waiting for a discharge after he was wounded abroad. He took me up to his home in Yorkshire. I lived up there, slept with his sister. We was up there eight months. They wanted to send me on a war climbing drill right out miles away so we decided we'd get married.

We booked a hall from the Co-op and we got as much food as we could. But flowers and fern we couldn't get, so we had to send to Ireland for that. All we done, we got married, went to the reception, had our photos taken, then went in the pub at night. My old man came up to Yorkshire, travelled up to give me away. Mum didn't come, I don't think she had the money. I had a blue wedding dress because his cousin got married in 1940 and she had a blue veil to go with her dress and they said "borrow something blue, it would be lucky". Mine was a lovely, long dress with three hearts on it. We didn't get extra coupons but he got a gratuity when he came back from abroad, plus he got a war pension after 1942.
*So you weren't hard up in the war then?*

Well, not really. Everyone seemed to have money, I don't know why.

## Work

Before I got married I worked in Stratford in a place called the Excel, a factory in Carpenters Road that made sausages and luncheon meat and things like that. We were putting sausages in tins to send to the troops, putting the oil in the tins to keep the sausages.

Oddly enough, we didn't seem to have a raid at work. I don't remember one. Our wages were about £2 a week whereas an average man that was any good earned a fiver. Conditions were bad. You had to be very quick on time. You only used to get a ten minute break. You used to have to drink your cup of tea or eat your bit of bread when you was working at a bench. Excel, being a food place, used to supply packs of pies and mugs of tea.

*Did you ever work on ammunition?*

No, cos it was too tedious. Putting little shells in....

After I was married I got a job in Huddersfield in a place where I was making jam, cutting the stalks off cherries and things like that. After that I got a job in a soap factory where Harold's sister worked. I stayed there for about two years.

## Back to London

First of all Harold did a bit of fire watching and he got so fed up just being married that he used to work every night and get one Saturday off every fortnight. He done that for six months then he got all fed up of it. He had to have a light drill and he had to do light work so he got a job in a factory oiling the machinery, but he didn't like that. Yorkshire was very different from London. There wasn't a lot of entertainment, it was dreary. So in 1944 we decided to come back to London.

We stayed at Angel Lane for a week and we got a house down Vicarage Lane for a pound a week. Mum and I each paid ten bob a week. A pound a week for an eight-roomed house! Then the woman next door moved away and I moved into the empty flat. We used to sleep on the kitchen floor on a mattress.

It was very difficult to get your bits together. Curtains was all rationed. You never had nettings. The toss-up was: say you needed to buy underclothes bad, would you buy the underclothes, would you buy the curtains? I did get a bed in the end at Vicarage Lane. Lucky it wasn't a new bed because all the wall fell on it. If we'd been in bed we would have got killed. That's what it was like, you see. You used to take a chance.

Harold got a job in the Forest Gate skating rink. Roller skating, shift work. He used to roll round on the skates and chuck anyone out who wasn't behaving. He couldn't do heavy work. He had a badge to say he was an ex-serviceman.

## Living with the bombs

The bombing was concentrated on the docks. Walking round at night your heart was on double. You used to have passwords, they were looking for spies and they'd come and shoot you if you didn't know the password. When the raids started you couldn't sleep in your bed. We used to take the dog down the shelter in the garden. Then we'd come out and see all the people hurt.

Harold walked round and saw some terrible things and he comforted people. People used to come to the doors to give them cups of tea. I didn't go out. I used to cry because I was nervous. But we had some good times as well, people were more sociable then. If you went into the pub everyone was nice and friendly and you would enjoy it, mixing with people.

When the raids came during the day everyone used to run and the stalls were all left unattended. Then after a while they started to get someone to look after them because people were thieving from the empty shops and stalls.

During the war sometimes I'd go over to my friend's house to sleep or she'd come to mine. We were in bed one night in Angel Lane and a land mine dropped four turnings away and we never even knew about it: great sleepers we were!

When Hilda came home from Devon she came round my house in Vicarage Lane and we were sometimes awake for three days at a time, walking round looking at the damage. We used to get so exhausted. When it first happened there wasn't wardens on the spot right away. You go past a shop and you see a tin of salmon. When the stalls were out you'd see apples and oranges. Then after a while it all got scarce.

We moved one night, before the war ended, from Vicarage Lane to Reeve Road. Hilda came with me to get some fish and chips. We were coming past Queen Mary's hospital. It had been hit by a doodlebug and there were people in the ambulances and children screaming, all covered in blood. I was pregnant and I cried and cried. We both cried. When I got home I was in a state and I couldn't eat the chips or anything.

## Pies and prejudice

There were Lyons corner houses where you could get food and you didn't have to put the ration coupons in. In the churchyard in Stratford there used to be a woman who'd sell pies, a coffee stall they used to call it. You could buy a sandwich and pies and they used to come down the shelter. She'd have a teapot set up in the shelter. Tea was tuppence a cup but the old cow used to sell small cups with no handles on them.

She wouldn't serve the blackies, she hated them. With the Jews, they used to have to serve them, couldn't refuse, they used to slap it at you.

*Did you hate the Jews? I mean, what about the Germans and the Jews?*

There was good and there was bad. Never met a German in my life, never really came across them to socialise. Mari, who had the shop next door, was a Jewess. Nice woman, she thought the world of me.

I was in a bus shelter once and the raid had started. You couldn't see anything because it was all pitch black. You weren't allowed to have lights. Even a little fag they reckoned the pilots could see from the sky. There was this bloke speaking to me. He had a beautiful voice and I thought to myself "He must be nice". Anyway the bombing got worse and across the road there was a proper shelter so we all went down there. When we got in he was a blackie. Everyone turned away. They wouldn't talk to him. English man, I think. He talked very educated. I felt so...when you see them with the light and all the people there, you felt really bad but you walked away and sat with somebody else. I just said "Excuse me, I think I know someone." He was as black as a newgates knocker, just come off the boat.

## Rations and the black market

We used to get three ounces of marge and about two ounces of cheese. Inside your book you had a coupon. Say you wanted a tin of fruit it would be about eight points and they'd take them out of your book. A lot of people used to run out, especially if they had families, but if you had a bit of money and you knew people you could use the black market. It was under the counter straight from the shopkeeper. It didn't do no harm but it was all illegal. We'd get it in the little places. In them days you had your little grocery shop or stall. They got whatever they could, but fruit got scarce, onions got scarce and meat, you couldn't get liver. That was off ration and that's why you couldn't get it. Then they started selling horsemeat. Yuk!

When they had a consignment and a lot come in all the people would queue up for it. Once there was a great big queue and I thought to myself "Sod that, I ain't going to bleeding queue round there because when it gets to me there might be none left". I was with Auntie Connie so I said I'd go and find out how much they'd got left. She said "You wouldn't have the nerve." I said "I bloody well will." So I went in there. Someone said, "Don't push in, mate." I said "I ain't bloody well pushing in. All I want to know is if they'll have enough left. I ain't going to queue round there like a lemon and when it get round they ain't got none left." This was about 1950. Stuff was still scarce by then.

There was one thing in the war that I hated and that was the bread. It was a khaki colour and the marge, yuk, like cart-grease. We used to have things called rissoles. Potatoes were four pounds for tuppence. You could cook a dinner for sixpence. When we moved into Vicarage Lane I never had a saucepan, I never had nothing. Cos you couldn't set up home on account of the raids all the time. I had no children then and Harold was at the skating rink so we'd just go out and have makeshift meals in cafes.

If you had plenty of money you could get anything you liked on the black market. You'd get in the know from talking to people and finding out who the spivs were. The spivs came into the pubs, into the shelters and in the park as well. He'd say "What do you want? I can get it for you." Even shops were doing it under the counter. Selling tea at half a crown a packet. Tea was usually only about fourpence a quarter, so they were making quite a profit.

## Fiddles

People were claiming money from the UAB for food and gas. There was also a fiddle going with mattresses. One person would have a damaged mattress, like it might be covered with ceiling plaster or something and the man would come round from the UAB to see if you needed a new one. Then the person would pass the mattress on to a neighbour so they could go to the UAB for a new bed as well and so on. I was only young then and I was all frightened and scared. I went up and they didn't give me enough so I come back and told Jimmy and he went up there and got some more.

## Deserter

I knew this girl in the ATS who was a military policeman, called Louie Buttroll. She deserted but she never got in touch with me. Then she come to Angel Lane and stopped there for a couple of days. We didn't know she'd deserted and the police come round, some of the army mob. They took her back. I don't know if she went in clink. I never heard from her. To be honest, I didn't like her a lot. After the war had finished I heard about her again. She moved down West Ham Park and she was with a fella with one arm. She had a kid before she got married. It wasn't the done thing, called a bastard. You'd be chucked out.

## Pregnancy

Used to be too frightened, me, to have a baby. Not because I was stupid but we never talked about sex. You didn't know nothing and therefore you got ignorant. So I said once to mum "what's it going to be like to have a baby?" Do you know what she said? "Why don't you bleeding have it and find out."

*So you didn't have any idea you were pregnant?*

No, not really. I was really ignorant about how babies were born because you were never told about that sort of thing. I thought they cut your stomach open to get the baby out. I had to sort of get it all together myself.

I got pregnant in 1945, about March. The doodlebugs were coming. I went to Forest Lane Hospital, it's still there. In them days people never made a habit of going to hospital. You go at three months, you go at six months. They'd send you bills and if you couldn't pay it right away, you'd have to pay so much a week. About £30 altogether.

During the war, with all the clothes being rationed, nurses never had any tights or stockings. You never had maternity shops either. I used to wear overalls. When you had the baby a woman used to come around, to check things out. A "lady in green" mum called her.

When bananas came in you'd normally have to queue but being a mother you got priority and expectant mothers didn't have to queue. Then people would say to me "Get me some of this and that". Even after the war things were rationed but you usually knew a neighbour who was hard up and she'd sell you a quarter of tea and things like that. Or you'd exchange with the neighbours.

# LEN
## running away

At the start of the war, when Len was 12, he and Hilda were evacuated to West Mersea. They were treated badly and Len ran away to Colchester. When he was found he was taken to a mental institution. His headmaster took him back to school and he and Hilda were moved to another billet. They returned to Stratford in November 1939 because the feared raids had not yet begun.

They were later evacuated again, this time with younger brother Ronnie to Devon. There were tensions at school, Len was treated badly at his billet and he ran away again. He was sent away to a workhouse. After more attempts to run away he was finally rescued by his father and returned to Stratford.

Len was fascinated by his father's stories of the First World War but found them difficult to understand: "It was all strange to me, blokes blowing each other up in trenches." Now he feels that youngsters are as bewildered by his tales of civilian deaths in World War II as he was by his Dad's memories of the first war.

*Evacuated children leaving London*

I was nearly 12 years old when the war broke out. I went to a huge elementary school near the Greyhound pub, opposite my grandmother's haberdashery shop. It was very strict and really you were bullied into an education.

## Unpleasant evacuation

Me and Hilda were sent to West Mersea with my school. A load of old-fashioned buses took us to Paddington Station where we was met by some people and ushered onto the train. There were planes flying over. Very likely they was there to protect the train. They was the RAF, following us, and they never left the train until we got to the country. Spitfires they were, protecting the train cos Jerry will come over and start on it. Of course, German fliers didn't know who was on the train and they would have attacked it.

When we got there they took us to this massive place. It was a rich woman's house but she didn't want us there for long. Next day, we were taken off somewhere else. A billeting officer turned up unexpectedly to say she was going to take us somewhere. The car had a bonnet with silver sides. It was a very old-type Vauxhall. Sometimes you see them now on the road, very occasionally.

We were taken to Mrs Gale's. Her old man was an ex-copper. Even his son didn't like him, a big old bully. We shared a bedroom with two other evacuated kids. When the other two told Mrs Gale they had the same surname as her she said "I don't care what your name is!" A couple of days after we got there she made this meal of salad and meat. There was all this lovely lettuce and cucumber on the table. I started telling her what sort of food I liked and didn't like but then she put this bread and jam in front of us. She said "That isn't for you, this is yours" pointing at the bread and jam. I thought "you old cow". Her son and her old man sitting up at the end of the table didn't even look at us. They didn't take pity on us and say "You look miserable, you look homesick. Do you want to come and buy sweets with me."

I was fed up with the situation at Mrs Gale's and decided to walk to London. In Colchester two coppers spoke to me. They said "We've been looking for you", and took me to the police station. I ended up in a mental institution called Severalls in Colchester. I had a tomato sandwich and a cup of Oxo and went to bed.

During the night one of the inmates woke me up, saying "Are you the new boy?" It frightened the life out of me. Breakfast was served in a room that contained forms and tables. Playtime was 'ring-a-ring-a-roses' played by adults, which I found amazing. I knew I was in a pickle. A nurse called me and I was taken to meet my headmaster, Mr King. He was small, wearing a trilby hat and smoking a pipe. He took me back to school, and then me and Hilda were taken to Mrs Johnson who had a place by the sea. We were really happy there, but Hilda told the teacher we was sharing a bed, and they all went mad. When we got home from school, the stuff was all packed and we were sent off somewhere else.

## Home for a while

Anyway, the war wasn't going on at home so Dad came and got us. We came back by charabanc. Dad got told by the billeting officer that it was a very stupid thing to do, but he came for us anyway.

I used to go down the shelter about seven o'clock at night. The old man and Harry stopped out and Jim was in the army. There was only me and my mother and the younger ones down there. We first started using the shelter when the Blitz was heavy, in 1940. We used to sleep down there. Terry was a baby and he kept me awake so one day I got annoyed and left the shelter. Walking through the yard I could see all the fires started by Jerry and there was a real smell of gunpowder. It was a proper battle. All of a sudden Jerry let one go and it blew all the windows out. Everyone was screaming. The old man came rushing out of the shelter. "All right?" he says. I was shaking, being in a big explosion like that.

## Evacuated again

Later on me, Hilda and Ronnie were sent to Devon. Ronnie and me stayed with Mrs Perry. The locals didn't like us at all. At school it was locals in the morning and evacuees in the afternoon. Most country people before the war hated Londoners. They had no time for us.

At school I had a fight with a Canadian kid. You know what Canadians are, still bigheads even now. A proper little git he was, sorting all the class out, and he thought he'd take a chance on me. "Want a fight, kid?"

"Get out of it, I don't want to fight you", and I pushed him away. Then, of course, we had a set-to and everyone was cheering. I was the hero of the school after that. Everything I done they were on for me. All the girls used to say: "What are you doing now, Leonard?" The girls were all lovely. Big hero of the school, I was, cos he was the bully of the school and they was all frightened of him. Even the teachers were cheering. I got the better of him. It made me feel good because I put him in his place. He was a thickset kid, I mean he banged me but I won.

## Sent away

The billeting officer come for me. She said "I'm taking you somewhere to get your eyes done for you. You've got very bad eyes." But she took me to this workhouse. I didn't know what it was, being a kid of only about 13. I waited in the car and a bloke with a white coat come along. "Come with me", he said. Not a very nice attitude, it put the wind up me. They took me to a ward with all old boys in it, very old men, 70, 80 odd. They said "That's your bed in the corner".

## Escape, capture and rescue

But as time went on I got out of there. There was a boilerhouse with all the coal leaning up this wall. I climbed over the wall and jumped over the other side. So I went to try to get information back home to the old man. I visited Mrs Perry and told her all about it. But then a bloke knocked on the door. "Leonard Shingler here?" he asked. Then he saw me. "What's this? You escaping?" He was in civvies, a detective or someone. As we walked along the road we bumped into a big policeman, a great big country copper. The first man explained "This boy is escaping from our institution" and the copper goes "Look here, you behave yourself. More of your attitude and you'll be going somewhere worse". I got real scared, I thought I was a prisoner.

So he took me back again and when we got back they took all my clothes off me and I couldn't go out or nothing. Eventually they gave me the clothes back and I could walk about the grounds of the workhouse. Late one evening I was standing by the gate. There was an old boy there, the gatekeeper. Suddenly someone shouted out "Is that you Len, Len is that you?" and it was my old man. Hilda wrote to our mum and she told my dad to come and get me. He says " Come with me, I want to see someone about this". So we went to the office and he says "I'm taking the boy home."

"You can't take him home. You have to go through the legal channels."

"He's coming home. Where's his kit?" and he says to me "Go pack your stuff".

So I went upstairs like a kid with a new toy – going home! When I come down I could hear the old man hollering and shouting in the office. Finally he comes out and says "Well, ready man?". He called me 'man', and away we went. I walked out the gate and I felt free again, it was marvellous.

## Stratford shelters

At home they used the crypt of St John's church at Stratford as a shelter. There was a woman down there selling pies and cheese and cakes. During the war you couldn't get food without queuing. So you only had a limited amount of food so anyone who sold food done a roaring trade. Stuff was very nice and appetising and you'd go down there and buy some cheese. All the cakes were laid out and behind them were the bodies buried in the wall. "Here lays..." all these old-fashioned names.

We only tended to use the public shelters if we were caught out. People who used them regularly used to book them up. They had bunks down the crypt to sleep in there all night. Those people were greedy, you know. As long as they were alright that was okay.

The other public place was the Central Line tunnel from Stratford station where the underground went to Leytonstone. That was under construction at the time and we had a regular place down there. People used to sleep in there waiting for the bombs. They were very haughty, the people down there, and unsociable, but maybe that was because we were kids. Our special job in the morning was to pick up all the bedding and make sure we didn't leave nothing behind.

One day there was a really heavy raid. That took place on 29th December 1940, two days before 1941. We was on our way to the tunnel. The guns were going off and everything was scaring the life out of us. All of a sudden the bombs started dropping through the air. I went in this house and it was shaking. Some bloke across the road said "Come on, come on, down here". So we all spent the night down his Anderson shelter. I don't know who he was. His missus and all his relations was down there. That raid was heavy, it was the Great Fire of London. Have you heard of that in history books? There was one in 1665 in the time of Charles II and this was the Great Fire of London in the time of Churchill, when the war was on. They set London alight end from end, but St Paul's wasn't touched. It was all round St Paul's.

After that I can remember getting the Anderson shelter for our own garden. When the war broke out everyone was issued with these Anderson shelters but apparently the council had a rush on them. Everyone wanted one and we was unlucky not to get one then. So Dad goes up to see the council after this bad raid. He was told there was one going at a certain street. The people had gone away and left it in the garden. Anyway we goes up and gets it and puts it up in our backyard. We pushed it back in a barrow.

## Remembering the war

I remember the raids, the flying bombs, the V2s, everything. The flying bomb was a thing that went through the sky. The engine would stop and it would float through the air. Sometimes it used to dive towards the ground. I was about 50 yards away from one once. It shook the ground. I was frightened, seeing all that black smoke coming up all over the building. I ran towards it to see what I could do but I was panicked as well.

Once a V2 rocket dropped when we were just about to have tea. The rocket came over the hill and all of a sudden it come down. We went to see what was up. You could smell the gunpowder and see the people with their houses all blown up.

You lot think I'm back in the olden days, don't ya? You don't know what I'm talking about. If someone told me about the first world war in those days I'd say "What's he talking about?" so I can understand how you feel. This war, though, I can remember every detail even though it was 50-odd years ago and it's in the history books.

My old man told me stories about the First World War, in the trenches and all that. I didn't understand but I was interested. It was all strange to me: blokes blowing each other up in trenches. This war was about blowing civilians up. Now in the First World War nobody was blown up. Just now and again you'd have a raid but this was almost every night. If Hitler hadn't gone and invaded Russia that would have been the end of London. You wouldn't be able to talk about the war, you wouldn't be here.

# HILDA
## city child, country child

Hilda was born in 1929. She was evacuated and spent much of the war in Devon.

Her story tells of the struggles and joys of leaving the city behind and learning to be a country child.

At 14 she returned to Stratford and started work in her mother's shop in Angel Lane, where she sold second-hand clothes and furniture.

She was 16 when the war ended and remembers the celebrations "up the other end".

By the time rationing ended in 1953 Hilda had two daughters of her own.

*Angel Lane, where Hilda worked in her mother's shop during the war*

We got on the train at Paddington and we all had labels on our coats in case we got lost. I didn't know any of the children, except my two brothers: Ronnie, who must have been four and Len who was 11 or 12. This was my second evacuation. Before that Len and me were sent to West Mersea, which was awful.

Anyway, after we got off the train at Devon we were put in a coach and taken to this church hall. There was tea and biscuits there and we were all sitting at these long tables, no table cloths or anything, just long wooden tables. It didn't matter who you sat with, you didn't know anyone. We all sat down and the ladies come round: "You want some tea, dear?" and biscuits and cake.

After that they said "Stand in a line, there are people going to come in and see you and take you to another place."

So in they all come and you were all standing there. It was like a jumble sale only they were buying children. They come up and look at you: "Hello, what's your name?" I had several offers but they only wanted me, just one girl. Len spoke up and said "No, she's with us, she's not going on her own. We want to stay together." So that's why I wasn't taken. Afterwards I knew the girl that was taken instead of me and it was a great life she had. It was a grocery shop and she had everything. I could have been there.

### Snow white sheets

We were the last ones left which was terrible, the only three left out of a train full of children. So Mr Whoever-he-was came up and said "Look, I don't know what we're going to do with you but we're going to take you now and find you somewhere nice to stay." The three of us sat in the back seat of the car and by this time Ronnie was going to sleep because he was only four and it was dark. We were a bit frightened but it wasn't too bad because I had my two brothers with me.

We pulled into this big place and a maid came to the door. She looked like something out of a book, with a white starched apron and a long dress and cap. "Come in, my dear, come this way." She took us to the kitchen. Oh, it was beautiful, all warm and sparkling, straight out of a television series, a big table and cooker. And she said "This be the cook" and the cook had big rosy cheeks, black hair, a fat woman. She said "Sit down. What do you want to eat? I bet you're hungry, aren't you?" I think we had cornflakes in a cereal bowl. Ronnie finished his and started to lick the plate so I smacked him: "Naughty boy, you're not to do that," and he cried. But I was like a mum to him, you see, I'd looked after him before. He didn't object to me smacking him, he just cried. So she said "Oh bless the little lad. Aren't you a proper little mother. I expect he's tired."

They took me to my little bedroom. I'd never seen anything like it in my life. The sheets were pure snow white and they put this hot water bottle in there as well. I had a wash first and the flannel was pure white and there were lovely towels. It was all warm. Then she combed my hair. I had long, curly auburn hair. My mum always said I had lovely hair and I think they were fussing round because of my hair. I had a nightdress or pyjamas in my little pack of clothes and I got into this bed. They tucked me in and everything. Oh it was lovely. Two of them come in and they were fussing about, "Isn't she lovely". That's the way they were talking.

The next morning they called me down to breakfast. Afterwards they said "Come and have a nice wash and dress. You're going to see the lady of the house." So they smartened us up and took us to this room. I didn't know what it was then but, thinking on it now, it was a big study with a big red carpet and a fire going and books all the way round. She was an old lady and she said "Good morning, how are you? Did you sleep well?" It was a little conversation, she was talking to us, "Where do you come from?" and all this. Then we went for a walk in the grounds of the house. It was like a park. She had one of those little long-haired dogs. She got us to throw the ball and the dog caught it. She was a lovely lady.

Then she took us back to the study and said "I've got three cards for you. I want you to write to your mum and dad to tell them you've arrived safely. Write what you want and I'll post them all." I wrote all the cards, just a few words on each: "Dear Mum and Dad, arrived safely". But then she said "look, you won't be staying here, dear. You're going to another nice place. I just put you up for the evening because a place couldn't be found for you, but somebody is going to come for you."

The man who came for us was a Salvation Army officer called Captain Holly. He was nice, he had glasses on. "Hello, what's your name? Where do you live? Would you like to come with me?" He took me by the hand and took us in a car to a Salvation Army hall right at the other end of the town. It was where they held the services, a great big old Victorian place and I was frightened. It was all empty and I thought "where are we going? what are we doing here?"

## Homesick and difficult

Captain Holly sat us down and said "I've got two nice young ladies coming". My brother said "What do you mean, two ladies? We want to be together." But Holly pacified him, "No, no, you'll be all right. You're only going to be living three doors away from your sister. Don't worry, you'll see her whenever you want." Then the door opened and in walked these two old ladies. One was short, a maiden lady and the other was married with a son of her own. The short lady was only about 4 foot 11 and I was frightened of her. She had a big hat on, a typical old fashioned lady for that time. He said to me: "This is the lady you're going to be staying with". I clung on to his coat because I was frightened of her and I didn't want to go. My two brothers went with the other one. I suppose they were both in their fifties but as a child you thought they were ancient.

Anyway we went from there and I walked along with my lady; my brothers walked with theirs, and she was playing with them, but my lady she didn't do nothing. So eventually we got home and she had a nice little house, spotless clean. We got in and she said "Want a cup of tea?" "No." "A biscuit?" "No, I want my mum. I don't want to stay here, I want my mum." She said "No, come on, you have to have something." It was all on a tray and tray cloth: two cups, a sugar basin, milk jug. Everything was nice. But I wouldn't have it and I sat there in a corner, cry, cry, cry. I wouldn't have nothing. It wasn't her fault, it was a shame really but whatever she tried to do I just cried and sat in the corner. It must have been about two hours and she didn't know what to do with me.

Then she went out and she came back with a girl who lived next door called Doreen. She was about 17 and she said "What's the matter with thee? Why are you crying?" and asked if I would like to go to the pictures with her. I stopped crying just like that. This girl took me to the pictures and bought me fish and chips. Oh, it was lovely. When we got to the gate I was going to start crying but she said "Now c'mon, don't be silly. She's a nice lady, you'll get used to her. Stop crying." So she gave me a pep talk and I went in and up to the spotless bedroom. You never had carpets then, it was lino, highly polished and there was a jerry under the bed with roses on it. I done a wee in it, like you did. You can laugh but everybody did that then, did a wee in a jerry just before you went to bed. My mum even did it.

So I got in and it was pure white sheets again. I'd never seen anything as white. It was a double bed with a big thick eiderdown, beautiful blue satin all done in flowers. And the lady, Miss Candy, came in and knelt down and said her prayers. I thought that was a bit strange because I had never seen it before. She didn't say them out loud, but she was saying her prayers. She had a night-dress on. I turned round to face the wall and she just got into bed with me and that was it.

The next day Doreen came and knocked for me to start school. She was my best friend and I gradually settled in. The only thing was, my lady wouldn't let me out to play so when I came in from school I would have to stay in. I used to cry but she wouldn't let me out. I think she was afraid, she didn't know anything about children, maybe she thought I would run away. I would look out the window and see all the other kids playing in the street.

Then one day there was a knock on the door and it was my dad, come down to see me. I was crying. He said "what's the matter?" and I said "she won't let me go out and play". So he said "go on, you can go out". With that it altered. I got out to play. Occasionally my dad used to send me a half crown postal order.

## Two little brothers

My brothers lived three doors away but I never saw much of them. Ronnie was too young to go to school and my other brother went to the boys' school. My school was an all girls' school. One morning I was going to school with Doreen and out come Ronnie with a big man's cap on and a big pair of old boots on. He was on his own. I asked him where he was going and he says "I'm going to school". He was only 4½ but they started him at school. So I took his hand and went to see his headmistress and started him at school. After that I took him every morning.

He had been a lovely looking boy with curls but all his hair had been cut off. It was what you call a crew cut now, but then it was called a lousy haircut, to get the louses out of your hair. He come to school one morning with sores all over his head and no hair. I took him to the headmistress and said "my brother needs to go up the clinic" so she said "all right Hilda, take him to the clinic in the morning". So I took him there and they dabbed these sores with red paint or whatever so now he had a bald head and red spots all over it. When I went up there with him the nurse lifted this scab up and showed me: "Look", she said, "he's got fleas underneath the sores". I reckon he must have had impetigo because years after I saw that in a child and you used to have to lift the scab and get it off.

He come out about half-three from school. If you had a little brother or sister in the infants you could go and get him and bring him into your classroom. So I used to go and get him every day and he would sit with me at my desk. These girls in my class used to say "eh, look at his head", but he wouldn't say a word. He was right down in himself, he would not say nothing. The teacher never spoke to him. You find that in life, if you look like that nobody's got no time for you. So this was beginning to get on my nerves. I was so old-fashioned I went to see the billeting officer, believe it or not. I was 11 years old and I said to her "please miss, my brother has got sores on his head and fleas. He must be living in a dirty place." The next news, I come home from school and my lady says "your brother's been taken away". They took him away to a place at Teignmouth. I never saw him for ages after that.

Anyway, then my mum come down visiting and she brought my younger brother, Terry, who must have been about 18 months or so – beautiful little boy, same curly hair as Ronnie, a sturdy little boy. Mum stayed at the place where Ronnie had been and the lady got round her and said "Leave the baby here, don't take him back to the bombing". So afterwards I used to knock on the door.

"Can I see my little brother?"

"Oh, he's asleep".

I don't know if Mum knew about the sores. I couldn't have told her because surely she wouldn't have left him there. I don't understand that bit at all. When you're a child nobody tells you nothing.

So, I didn't know nothing about Terry. I hardly saw him and yet when he was a young baby I used to feed him, give him bread and milk, practically brought him up. Then I come home one day and my lady said "You're little brother's gone away into hospital. He was so ill he was passing blood."

I don't know what she done with him. I never saw him in the hospital. Then I was told that when he got better they put him in a place called Ashley Court, about two miles outside Tiverton. So I kept on agitating, "I got to go and see my brother", but I was told I wasn't allowed. Well, you know what I done? I went to the billeting officer and I said to her: "I want to see my brother. He's been put away and I don't know where he is." Now she was a nice lady to talk to. In them days they used to wear an official uniform, a certain colour costume and a big green hat, so you knew who they was. She said, "Well, Hilda, I know where he is. I'll give you the address. You can go and see him."

You couldn't get a bus so I walked it, two miles. It was a big house, Ashley Court. There were lots of little babies there and nurses walking around. I said "I've come to see my brother". They asked who he was, I told them Terry Shingler and then they went and got him. Well he was lovely then, a little fat boy, but he could not say a word. Nowadays, you would say he was retarded - he was two or three, but he could not say a word. They never gave me nothing when I went there, not a cup of tea, but I would stay all the afternoon. I would play in the grounds with him or run wherever he run. He used to act silly. You know what little boys are. And I remember I used to have a watch, and that's the first word I taught him. "Watch, listen, tick tock, tick tock", and he used to go "tick tock, tick tock." He was spoilt rotten there. He done whatever he wanted, but bearing in mind, I think, it was a babies' home and he was the oldest one there so he wasn't playing with children of his own age, just little babies. I don't know what it was for this place, evacuated babies maybe, nobody told me.

So I used to go there regular, every Saturday afternoon. I wouldn't even go swimming with my mate but walked two miles there and two miles back. I heard later that one of the nurses there wrote to my mum saying she wanted to adopt him. She thought he was lovely. My mum wrote back apparently and said "no". Anyway, everybody there thought he was lovely, even the matron. He used to go up to her and pull her frock.

This went on for some time, me going every Saturday, but one day the matron said to me, "Look, I don't want you coming here anymore. You're not allowed here". What did I do? I went to the billeting officer and she said, "You go whenever you want to. He's your little brother, you go and see him". And I did.

When he was school age, about five I suppose, I was told he had been taken away from Ashley Court and put with Ronnie at Teignmouth. So I never seen them two again for ages and ages. And that was the end of that.

### Life with Miss Candy

Miss Candy was a maiden lady and, although I didn't know this as a child, she was on what you would call now social security. It had a different name then. We used to call it the U.A.B. in Stratford – the Union Assistance Board. Well, every Tuesday I was told "Cut that out now, Mr Kemp will be here in a minute." Mr Kemp, oh, he was a miserable man! He used to pull up in his car and of course you never used to see cars then, but he had a red car and would get out and bang, bang on the door. He would walk in, "Morning", and put her money on the table, bang. She had a polished table because she was very house proud. She had to say "Thank you" and then "Bye" and off he'd go. He never spoke, never asked "how are you?" Never spoke to me, never spoke to her. But it was strange that instead of her going to collect the money he used to bring it to her every Tuesday, dead on time, dead on the door nail. That was her money and what she got I can't tell you. She also got money for me. She had a book for me, and drew it out every Thursday. She'd make a day of that. Thursday was her shopping day. She'd go up the town and get her shopping with her ration. We used to call it "go get the rations".

I wasn't allowed a key, so if she was late I used to have to wait at the gate until she come back. I was never allowed in the house alone. I was there for four years and was never allowed in unless she was with me. Whether she thought I was going to pinch anything I don't know. One day a week, I think it was on a Tuesday, she went round to her sister's and I had to wait outside. Sometimes I went round to her sister's and waited for her in there but I found that very boring. I don't think her sister liked me anyway, which was understandable. They didn't want strange kids in their house. The sister's husband was a magistrate and he wouldn't say a word to me, never.

I remember once how me and my mate was walking along and you know how it is with your mates – you'd be laughing and giggling. Anyway when I got back Miss Candy said, "My sister saw you acting silly in the town. She thought it was disgusting, laughing and giggling like a baby. My sister said it showed her up." There was no love lost.

We always went round there at Christmas because Miss Candy lived on her own but her sister was married and had grown-up children and she took an awful lot of notice of what her sister said. On Christmas Day you sat down and there was a big table with all crystal on it, all poshly done, table napkins, the lot. You would have your dinner. The grown-up sons and daughters would be there. One daughter had a little boy. He was horrible, I hated him. One of these boys who could do whatever he liked: he used to hit me all the time, but I wasn't allowed to hit him back. Nasty little boy.

Anyway, there would be a Christmas present wrapped up on your plate, and you would open it before your dinner and it would be a pair of socks, white ankle socks. That's all you got. So then you would have to say "Thank you very much for the present". You sat there all day on a chair and one of them used to play a piano and you sang Christmas carols. Then you went home. There was no drinks, not like a good Christmas. It was all too old for me, I was only a child.

Miss Candy had lived with her mum and dad until they died. Looking after them, she had never got married. There was a whacking great picture on her wall, I'll never forget it, it was nearly as big as the wall and there was mum and dad, a little man with a beard, mum had a big hat on. The mum was sitting down on this old fashioned thing and he was standing behind her with his hat in his hand. It was a black and white picture. She had another brother who lived in Bournemouth but she never saw him. She seemed to be the only one out of the family who had stayed and cared for mum and dad.

Now, obviously there was no television then and we never had a radio. Other people did, the girl next door, they had a radio. Never bought a paper. I didn't know what was going on in the world at all. I didn't know anything about London, nothing about the bombing.

## A Devon child

Looking back, it wasn't such a bad life, I suppose. I had loads of friends.

**I settled in nicely, I spoke Devon; half the people wouldn't believe I was an evacuee. I was just like a Devon child.**

There was a river near us, River Exe. We used to go there every Saturday afternoon, a load of girls. We used to enjoy it, it was a right laugh. There would be cows there but we just swam anyway, we'd ignore them. They would stand there and watch you, but you weren't frightened. This was part of being a country child: you just swam in the river, and whoever it belonged to never minded. Not like nowadays. You wouldn't touch the cows, you wouldn't annoy them. They was just there and no child would hurt them.

I couldn't swim, I'd never even been in the water before until I went there. Somebody gave me an inner tube for a car. It was a whacking great thing. "Put this on you and you'll be able to swim." So there I was, I used to take this with me and blow it up, a big old black thing it was. And one day I was swimming with this thing and I got out of the water and it was flat. So therefore I could swim, but I hadn't known it. So then I could swim with the best of them.

**Money**

Miss Candy never had a lot money, she couldn't have done. I was kept clean, I had everything I needed to eat, but I never, ever had any money. I had this two and six postal order from my dad but I didn't get it every week. Sometimes I would get a letter, but I didn't always get the money. It might be every three or four weeks. I couldn't think to myself, I'm getting paid Friday.

It was a penny to go swimming, so if I didn't have my money I couldn't go. This girl said to me, "Do you want to go swimming?" I said "I can't, I haven't got a swimming costume." She said "I know a girl whose got one who might give it to you". It was a red woolly swimming costume and it must have had about 60 holes in it, or more. I sat down one night and I sewed every hole up. And that was my costume.

I could only go swimming in the proper swimming baths when I could pay for myself. One Saturday my mate said to me, "get up early and we'll go swimming. I'll see you in the morning." I said to my lady, "Have you got a penny?" "No, I haven't got any money, no." I cried and I cried and I cried, but I still didn't get the penny. So she said, "Right, I've had enough of you, I'm getting the billeting officer down to you. I'm going to throw you out. I'm fed up with your moaning and crying." So down the billeting officer come, she was there when I got back from school. She said, "We can't have this. Your mum and dad are at home and there's bombs dropping all round them." The way she said it, I started to cry, she frightened me. Oh, I thought, my mum and dad are going to get killed. I'd never thought of it before. What she said was horrible. "You behave yourself, you be a good girl." And I was crying. All this for a penny! I must have been frightened of the billeting officer. Had a big red nose, and a suit on, and talked posh. And of course when you're a child you're frightened of posh people. You think, oh God, they're going to take you away.

I had this doll from my mum and dad for the previous Christmas. They sent it not to my lady but to my brothers' lady. The idiot brought it down to me before Christmas and said "Look your mother sent you this doll." She should have kept it for me for Christmas day. But anyway I called her Shirley Sheila Shingler. Now there was only me and Miss Candy so it sat on the settee and never got touched. I used to knit her doll's clothes. She was my baby, I loved her. A bald-headed doll, never had any hair.

One day I was desperate for money and the woman next door to me had loads of children so I said to her "Do you want to buy my doll for two shillings?" And she bought it off me and gave me two shillings! How wicked! She should have said, "oh, no." So I had two shillings and that was like a fortune. I used to go to school and count my money. I'd say to myself "shall I buy some sweets or shall I save up for that?" That's why I'm so frugal, I've always been like it, ever since I was a kid.

As for clothes, Miss Candy couldn't get me any so I went to the billeting officer and said: "I need a pair of shoes badly. I haven't got any shoes." She sent me to this place in the town where they fit you out for clothes. I got a skirt, a jumper, a pair of shoes and a couple of pairs of socks. You wore ankle socks in those days. I never had such a thing as stockings, although my friend did and I was very jealous of her in the winter when I had thin little ankle socks on and the snow was six inches deep. You'd walk through the snow to school and you'd be sitting there all day with wet socks. Nobody cared, nobody took no notice at school. I got awful chilblains, they was hanging off me. I had to go to the clinic and have them dressed every morning. I could barely walk, agony it was. The clinic was right up at the other end of town and I had to go there every morning and then go to school. I didn't stay home from school. I was in dire agony but I still had to walk to the clinic every morning.

They never had a coat to fit me at this place so Miss Candy said "the woman across the road has got a coat to fit you". Oh my God, it was a big old granny coat with big flaps hanging off! It was like a 1920s coat. This woman put it on me and said "I'll take it up for you and put a hem in it." I cried, I wouldn't wear it. She said, "Well, if you don't wear it, that's your fault you'll get cold." They all took the rise out of me at school: "Where did you get your coat?", you know what girls are. I had to wear it, I had nothing else.

## A fast reader

In the dark, winter nights I couldn't go out to play. It was all countrified round there so we couldn't go out in the dark and the cold. So I read an awful lot. I couldn't afford to buy books. There was a girl opposite and she had every book under the sun. She was an only child and was spoilt, so if I wanted any books I knocked for it. She thought I liked her but I only went there for her books, I know its horrible, but it's true.

There was a nice library, a very old building up the town. You were only allowed two books and I would have them books read in only two nights. I just used to sit and read all night by the fire. One time when I took the books back this library assistant said "You haven't read these already." I said "I have" but she wouldn't believe me. "I'm not taking these books back! Don't come back for another week. I don't believe you." That was it, I had nothing to read. I was close to tears actually. But then there was nobody who used to look out for me. If it was my children I would go up there and say: "Look here, you mind your own business about them books", but I had nobody so I was near to tears over it all. I must have been bored stiff that week, because I was a great reader.

## The black soldiers

We had what you would call a recreation ground not far from our school. These girls in our class said to me and my friend, Monnie: "Why don't you come over to the rec tonight? It ain't half good over there. There's a load of Black soldiers. It's really good, you can talk to them and laugh". I said, "No, we better not, we could get into trouble", but Monnie said "We'll go!" So we went over there. I never knew anything about racism or anything like that.

They seem to be encased. They had this barbed wire all around. They were in an enclosure of criss-cross wires. You talked to them from outside the enclosure. You went up and they would come over and talk to you. They used to show off. They were only young, 18 or 19. I don't know why they were there, unless they were going to be shipped out. They were American. They wore Yankee uniforms and they were all Black. But I didn't think to myself "There aren't any White people here." I didn't think like that. I thought they were nice actually, but you couldn't get near them because they weren't out in the park, they was in this enclosure. There was one called Isaiah Perry. Every time we went over there Isaiah would always come and talk to me, and Monnie would have her bloke, well not really her bloke, but someone to talk to.

Anyway, I went up the shops or something and I was walking along and all of a sudden there was the policeman. They called him Bobby Jones. "Mornin' Mr Jones". He got off his bike and said "I want a word with thee. You've been over the park, haven't thee, with the Black soldiers?" I went bright red and I was frightened. He said: "You're not to go over there anymore. You've been seen. I don't want you going over there with the Black soldiers. You hear me now?" And with that he peddled away. He went to Monnie's house as well and her mum gave her a good hiding. She weren't allowed to go round with me anymore. But we sat next to each other at school. She said "My mum says I'm not to go with you anymore. She don't like Londoners anyway."

"But it was your idea."

"Yeah, but I didn't tell my mum that, I would have got another hiding, so I made out it was you."

We still used to go out, but we never went over to the rec again. We were too frightened, thought you could get put in prison for that, you see.

Another time there was a parade in the town, with the little soldier cadets, 16 year olds. As they were marching along one winked at me. Oh, he was nice, about 15 or 16. I don't know how she found out but later Monnie said "He wants us to meet him in the pictures on Saturday afternoon, he's going to bring his friend." We turned up at 'The Electric' and sat down next to him. He gave me a cigarette. I'd never had a fag before, and I was so frightened that I put a coat over me, but I smoked it. He put his arm around me but I took it away because I was too frightened. Everybody knew everybody and I was scared somebody would have told Miss Candy.

## Church and the other army

Miss Candy was a very religious woman and I went to church three times a day on Sundays. I went to Sunday morning church and in the afternoon to Sunday School when she went for bible class. And when Sunday school was finished I used to have to knock on the door where her class was. Miss Hayden who ran it would have a big hat on and she wore choker beads. I would go in but oh, it was boring. I couldn't understand it. I used to watch her beads going up and down. One Sunday Miss Hayden asked me, "Do you sing hymns at school?" I said "Yes", because I was always singing, loved singing, fancied myself as a singer. "Would you like to sing us a song?". So every Sunday afternoon she would say, "Hilda is going to sing us a nice song" and I would stand up with all the old maids and the old grannies and I would sing. "Beautiful, oh Hilda, beautiful." So I didn't mind going then, because they all loved my singing.

My friend at that time said "You ought to come to the Salvation Army. It's lovely up there." So I went up there with her, not telling Miss Candy. Captain Holly was there. I loved it all, the singing, the band, "Joy! Joy! Joy!", and all this business. It was in the afternoons as well so I went there instead of going to church. Miss Candy found out and she was going to throw me out over it. Murder, there was. But I loved it so I stuck to my guns and changed to the Salvation Army. I used to go in the night-times as well. But saying that, there was nothing else to do anyway. It was somewhere to go and my friends were all there.

## Len gets rescued

My brother, Len, the oldest one, he wasn't getting on down there. He lived in three or four different places and then my dad came down to get him. Now my dad was the type who wouldn't bother to take you out. He liked to go into the pub and drink cider. So he'd give you money and say "Here you are, Hilda, you and your mate can go to the pictures, buy fish and chips." She used to love it, my mate. So her and me went out and the next morning he was going to go home, back to London and he was taking my brother. There was a little tiny station there, what you don't get now, it was called a halt station. On that particular morning I didn't have to go to school because my dad said I could go to the station with them. So I went to the station and I cried: "I want to go home,

I don't want to stay here". "Oh come on Hild", he said. He would always call me Hild. "You're all right where you are, you've got your friends." I was crying and crying and along came the train and they got on it and waved. Even to this day I can't stand waving goodbye. I cried all the way home and by this time it would be about 12 o'clock. Miss Candy said "You can go back to school this afternoon."

"Don't want to go back to school."

"You can go back to school."

So I was really weepy, just couldn't get over it, but I went to school. Sometimes at school you'd all be in the classroom and the teacher wouldn't be there. You'd all be messing around and acting silly. This day all I done was sat and put my head on the desk and cried. There was this big, fat girl who was a Jewess, called Leah. She had a whacking great chest and never wore a bra. She used to wobble when she ran. She leaned over and said "What's the matter?" and she was trying to make me laugh, acting silly. She was going "Illy shally, illy shally" and with that the desk went over. All the class went quiet. Now when the teacher came we had to stand up and say "Good morning, Miss Norman". She was horrible, this teacher, not just to me, to everybody. Anyway, in she walked and the desk was on the floor. You had ink wells then and that was all over the floor. I was still crying and nobody knew what to do. "What's going on in here?"

One of the girls says "Please miss, Hilda and Leah have knocked the desk over."

So Leah stands up. "Please, miss, Hilda's dad went back this morning and she's crying."

"Go and get a bucket of water and scrub that floor, and don't get up until you've got it all off. I've never heard of such a thing."

So there I was with the bucket of water, scrubbing the floor, crying. And she never, ever said, "what's the matter?" I felt like Cinderella really.

I used to wet the bed. Miss Candy had beautiful beds, and I didn't tell her I used to wet the bed. I was too frightened. But I had this big rubber sheet and a draw sheet over like they have in hospital and that sufficed. She never moaned about it because it didn't effect the bed. I didn't always do it. By this time I was put into the other bedroom, in a single bed on my own. So I didn't piddle on her anyway.

When I was 12 they took all the evacuee children away camping for a week. I didn't know any of these children, the girls in my class never went. The weather was shocking. It rained and it rained, so we couldn't have tents and we stayed in a hostel. It was like a big house with a dormitory. I had to take my rubber sheet with me. You had to make your own bed up every night. I would lie awake half the night. I was terrified to go to sleep. But I never done it, so that was all right. Nobody knew and I was friendly with all of them. I had a nice time there.

On the Saturday morning you had to get all your things packed up, fold up all your sheets and blankets and tidy the place up. Now the rubber sheet I was doing fell on the floor and some girl came along: "Oh look! Somebody piddles the bed." They kicked that rubber sheet all over the room! And I did with them! It was mine but I was too ashamed to tell them. When they all went to breakfast I quickly folded up the rubber sheet and put it in my case and nobody ever knew. And you know it was a funny thing, I never done it any more after that.

## Old enough to face the bombs

In 1944 I was 13. You break up from school in July and I was going to be 14 the following week. So I knew that when I left school I could come home. Or if I didn't I would stay there and get work. I knew Miss Candy wouldn't get any more money for me, so I would have to earn my keep. My friend next door, Doreen, begged me not to go. "Stay here. We'll go to work together." But I was all fired to go: "No, no, no, I'm going back to London."

So my mum came down and got me. When I came home the war was still on. It was the time of the flying bombs. The warning would go and you could hear an aeroplane going over your head. It looked like a toy aeroplane with smoke coming out of the tail. Now if that stopped, the engine cut out, that meant it was going to drop like a bomb. It was a bomb with wings. As soon as the engine stopped we'd all be frightened. "Quick, quick, its going to drop."

Me and my mum used to go to the pictures all the time. A warning would go but nobody took notice. It would come up on the pictures: "A warning has gone. There is a warning" but nobody left, they just sat there and watched the picture. One particular time me and my mum went to the pictures at West Ham Lane, Stratford. The warning had gone. We was getting our tickets at the pay-box and there was this man behind us. Then over came the aeroplane, the flying bomb. And it stopped. We didn't know what to do. There were about six steps leading up to the cinema and this man said "Lay down, quick!" So we laid on the stairs, the three of us. Then you heard it: crash! and then silence. Oh, it was an eerie feeling. Outside there was a circle of flowers, like a green, right outside the Greyhound pub and on this circle was a fire, like the remains of a bonfire. This thing had just disintegrated on impact. The Greyhound pub was gone, all just rubble, and there were bodies lying all over the place. I remember seeing this woman in a flower cotton dress laying on her stomach. She had long black hair. It was raining on them. It must have been in the summer because none of them had a coat on. Me and my mum were first on the scene. Then along came the ambulances and police and a load of activity. But before that happened some men drew up in a lorry, an open topped thing, and they were picking all these bodies up and putting them in this lorry. They must have been dead because they were holding them by their arms and legs.

My dad was in the ARP, the rescue service, and he come along. He went up to my mum and she said, "Where have you been? Look, all these poor people laying dead." He said "I've just come back from Chingford, a trolley bus got a direct hit and it was so bad they just had to shovel the bodies out." And then said, "Go on, home! Standing watching all this!" And obviously, we didn't go to the pictures, did we?

We were never actually bombed out. A lot of Angel Lane went and we lost the shop windows. The bomb blast killed the cat and the kittens. We used to have this black and white cat called Jim. When the windows got blown out it killed her but that was about it, nothing else happened to us.

## Mum's shop

I was 14 when I come back from Devon. I was a nice little girl cos down there I'd been well brought up, please and thank you, a very nice well mannered girl.

To set the scene at home: there was the shop and what you call the shop parlour, and a door led off to the living quarters. You never had living rooms then, it was called the kitchen where the sink was and everything else was called the scullery. It wasn't posh like, you walked down the passage and there was the scullery, three bedrooms upstairs, no bathroom, lavatory in the yard. When I got in me mum was sitting in a chair and there was a man in the kitchen with a big sack of clothes. I didn't know then but he was called 'the man from Romford'. He took the bits out one by one, shook them and held them up. Mum sat and nodded with a fag in her hand and he put them down in a pile. Once he'd got them all out there was a big pile of clothes and nice pieces. I didn't say nothing, I didn't know what was going on. Then they haggled about a price. I don't know what she give for them. When he went she said "sort through them, Hild, and you can have what you want." Christ, there was satin pyjamas and blouses. I thought I was in heaven, never did have many clothes, even in Devon. After that my mum said she didn't want me to go to work, she wanted me to stay and help her in the shop.

Blokes would go out, usually every day, with a barrow. They used to hire a barrow and a board and they'd shout out "any old rags". People would bring out all their old rags in a big sack. Loads of men done it who weren't at work. It was an extra couple of bob. All them sacks, they sorted 'em out. Around the corner was a big rag yard, where they buy it by weight, but if they were nice they keep 'em to one side and sell 'em to my mother.

They'd come to my mother. We had nicknames for 'em all. There was two brothers who looked alike, we called 'em the Corsica brothers. They'd all come in the shop and say "all right, Rose?" but she wouldn't just buy the sack off 'em. They'd have to take everything out, shake each piece and show 'em to her. If she wanted it she'd nod and it would go on the floor.

My mum was very cute. She didn't price 'em up or anything. From the floor upwards there was clothes, clothes, clothes everywhere. You couldn't get in the shop sometimes for the clothes. So then in would come the women, sorting out the clothes. I used to be in the shop all day. Some woman would come in: "Have you got a frock to fit me, dear?" or "Have you got a coat to fit me, dear?" I could look at a person and tell what could fit 'em, I got that experienced at it. Some of 'em wouldn't ask you. It would be like a jumble sale, only more so. They'd sort out a load of bits and say to me or me mum "How much?". Then me mum would say "That's a shilling and that's twopence" and all this business. Clothes were on a ration then, you couldn't buy them except with coupons. People were glad to get the stuff. Women would be buying things for their daughters that were at work. Everybody would buy, cos it was handy. All the old girls come in. It was a really chatty affair, like a bleeding social club, come in and talk about the old man, "My old man's left me", all about their sons. You knew everybody's business. They'd say "Hilda, find me a frock" and I used to have to climb all over the clothes. I would shout out "Who wants this nice coat?" "Show us", and they'd grab it and look at it with one hand. They were always sniffing, purse in their hand, never had hand bags, and they'd hold it up and shake it and say "you reckon that would fit me, Hilda?" and I'd say "Yeah, go on, try it on". They couldn't try dresses on but coats and that.

Every now and again I would sort things out and if I thought it wouldn't sell, I used to sack it up and take the barrow. This was me, mind, a girl, and I'd push it all through the street to the rag yard. He would weigh the bag and give you so much a pound for it.

My mum would buy anything that she thought would sell. She'd buy furniture, she had pianos. We had an old boy working for us called Nat. He was a bit on the backward side but he did odd jobs for her and he was handy. He used to deliver the furniture for her on a barrow. When my mum bought a piano they always used to call it a deal: "I got to go and look at a deal". I used to go with her sometimes. If she bought a piano they'd go and get it on the horse and cart, me dad and me brothers. They'd put it in the wide forecourt of the shop and Nat could play like a dream. He'd sit in the street and play that piano and she'd have it sold in an hour. They would all come around listening.

I remember one time this woman's mother had died or something and she had to get everything out of the house, cos otherwise she would still have to pay the rent. So they cleared the whole house out, everything just as it stood, and they put it all on the forecourt. There was chests of drawers filled up with stuff, everything from the house. I thought it was great. I stood there all day with people looking at this and that: a side board, a chest of drawers, kitchen utensils and God knows what else. No word of a lie, there were a hundred people around there looking. But my mum done it silly, half of it got nicked. They all took it out and put it in their pockets. We didn't have enough hands to serve 'em. We didn't know what we was doing. It was silly but you couldn't tell my mother: "Don't tell me what to do", she'd say.

The stuff she used to get in there... antiques, she didn't know what antiques was really. Caught blind she was. There used to be a Jewish man come in who would buy all the men's sports jackets. He come with a big sack and he'd buy 'em all. My dad found out that he had his own factory and he was making caps out of her stuff. Dad had a row with her, saying "you're not all there. He's making a bomb out of you through all that material". But she said "you mind your own business" cos it was her own shop, see. He was right in a way because she should have charged him a bit more, but she never, she just sold all these jackets as ordinary coats.

Another thing she used to buy was pawn tickets. That was great. She used to send me to go and get 'em. They were all poor then and so you pawned your old man's suit. A lot of the men never even knew. They'd take the suit in and give you a ticket and, say, half a crown. That was a lot of money. If you wanted to get it out again you'd have to pay, say, another sixpence on it. Sometimes a family wouldn't have that money to get that pawn ticket out, but if you wanted to keep it you had to go and give them so much a week till you could afford the whole amount. So a lot of 'em used to sell the pawn ticket cheap, cos otherwise you'd lose the suit in pawn and you wouldn't get a penny. So they'd sell it to my mum for so much. Then she'd say to me "take this ticket up to the pawn shop" and I used to come back with a big parcel, all bits and pieces. A lot of it would be sold in the shop. Some of it was good stuff in those pawn parcels.

You name it, she had it, she'd buy anything. But she stopped buying bikes because she bought a bike off a young boy and the coppers come in and said it was stolen. Mum lost the money when they took the bike off her. So she wouldn't take a bike unless she had a note from the parents. That was a laugh because some of them would want a receipt, but there'd be no writing paper so you'd tear the front out of a book and write on that.

My mum made a good living out of it. The time came when I was sick and tired of it all. This girl, Joyce, who I knew before I was evacuated, came and knocked for me. She never spoke to me when I came home. Of course we were like strangers cos four years is a long time in a kid's life, But one day she came in the shop and said "are you looking for a job?". "No, not really" I said. "Do you want to come out with me tomorrow and look for work?" so I said "yeah, all right then" and I never bothered any more but I was still in on Saturdays .

When I was married and had the children I still used to go out there and serve. Mum would say, "Do us a favour, go and see what that old cow wants". The door had a glass window and you could see from there. She'd say "Oh she don't want nothing", and the woman would stand there for an hour and would buy nothing. But you had to stand with her, it was a nuisance. Then we had Jill Large who came in every week. She had a whacking great swirled foot and she'd say "I have got a big hoof. Did you find that other shoe?" We nicknamed her Big Hoof.

I also had a stall. It was my brother's idea. They set me up with a horse and cart and I had this clothes stall. I think it was in Rathbone Street. I was doing pretty well, I had my own customers. But then my mum wouldn't let me have any more clothes. She said "leave them, I can sell them here". I said "can I not have my own raggies?" – we called them raggies – and she said "no you can't". So I never had my stall anymore. But I used to sell kettles with my dad on the horse and cart. We had a stall at Romford on Wednesdays and Saturdays, Woolwich was Tuesdays and Fridays. I used to stand and say "Here you are! One and

36

fourpence halfpenny a four-pint kettle. All sound, no leakers."

## Theatrical ambitions

The shop was on the corner of William Street and Angel Lane and there was a sort of backyard down William Street. My mum used to let the window cleaner put his barrow in there and only charge him half-a-crown a week. Anyway the Theatre Royal was in a street opposite the shop and my mum did an advert for them, a big bill poster on the wall advertising what was at the Royal. At that time it was all variety. During the war everywhere kept open, nobody took notice of the war.

So consequently, for having this bill on the wall, we got two free passes to go to the Royal and generally me and my mum went. I used to love it. We could sit in the front row, the most expensive seats in the house. The band was in the little bit just down from the stage and I used to sit there and get off with the drummer. Oh, he wasn't half nice! He used to wink at me and all that. I would make out I wasn't interested like you do, but I really fancied this drummer. I only went to see him. That's as far as it went. He used to wink at me but nothing else happened.

Then my dad got a job there scene shifting and he had to go there every night. So I could go over to the Royal any time I liked through the stage door. I used to go there and stand in the wings all night, watching the chorus girls. They had a shocking life them chorus girls. One of these women had a troop of chorus girls and she asked my dad if she could have me in her troop. My dad said no and when he told me afterwards I said "why did you say no, I wanted to go" and he said "you don't realise the life they have". They would finish up on the Saturday night and on the Sunday they'd be travelling all night to the different theatres all over England. At night half of them would be sleeping together. Then on Monday they'd be back on stage again. They'd have no time for themselves and no money.

There was this talent competition going on and I went in for it, off the top of my head. They asked people from the audience to go in for it then and there. So I got up on the stage because I used to sing in the pub and I fancied myself as a singer. I sang 'If you ever go to Ireland'. I'm not kidding, I brought the house down. I got into the finals which was going to be on the Friday night. I couldn't eat or sleep for a week for the excitement. Anyway the finals came, with the winners from every night. I sang the same song and this old man came on after me. He was the silliest old sod. He was wearing white slippers and he was really old, white hair and everything. He wasn't doing anything but everybody was laughing at him. And he won it! I should have won it. It was disgusting, he wasn't doing nothing. But then I got to the finals, which was something.

I also sang in the Lion pub on Angel Lane, just about three doors away from where I lived. There was a little raised thing in the pub and on it was a piano and drums. The bloke on the drums was in the Air Force. It was during the war but he would come back occasionally on leave. Of course, everybody there would give a song, that was how it was. A glass of ale was sixpence and you'd sit down and that ale would last you all night. So you had a good night out for sixpence. There was no dancing allowed: they didn't have a licence for dancing, but they'd all sing. When I used to walk in the pub the bloke would play 'I'm a little on the lonely side', because that's what I used to sing.

I wasn't old enough to go in a pub, but they never knew that. I was about 15 but I looked older. The bar owner was a big fat woman, full of swank, and her man had stomach trouble and all he could drink was milk. He used to have a glass of milk on the bar. She sat there all night on her stool and never done a thing. But he would say to my father "She's got a nice voice, Harry, your daughter. You ought to go further with that". But my dad took no notice. He was showing off when I first won but when I didn't win the final he never mentioned it again. I was a good singer, I'll say that myself. I loved show business. What I should have done, was do it myself anyway, but you never had any opportunities, never had any money, what could I do?

## After the war

*What was it like at the end of the war?*

It was a normal day actually. Everyone was at work as far as I can remember. The church bells were ringing and, of course, you heard it on the radio. You never had television then. What day did it end, the war? I can't remember but on the Saturday I went up the other end, up Leicester Square and that, with some bloke I was going with and up there was packed solid. Everybody was 'Knees up Mother Brown' and all that, and drinking. You never had canned drinks then, it was bottles of beer. When I come home again there was a street party on William Street.

Somebody had a piano in the street and this sailor asked me to dance. He was quite nice as well but I fell all over him because I couldn't dance. I felt a right Charlie. He didn't ask me any more. It was waltzing, and 'When the lights go on again, all over the world', slow dancing. They didn't have any rock 'n' roll then or anything like that, jitterbug was in. Big band sound, you had at that time.

They must have had the children's street party on the Saturday afternoon. My little brothers went to but I didn't take any notice of that. They had long tables right the way down the street and they must have had a collection because they sat all the kids down to eat. In the night somebody had the piano in the street and everybody was dancing. I didn't like it much, it got on my nerves. When you're that age you don't want to sit with those old grannies, so I went indoors.

I remember one day after the war when the King and Queen and the two girls come through Stratford. They were small, Margaret was near my age. They went right past the old town hall in an open-topped car. They went all around the East End like a victory parade. That Princess Margaret had the bluest eyes I ever seen, oh they was blue. I just stood and stared at them. Everybody was going "ah, ah, ah" and had flags.

Things went from bad to worse after the war. The war ended and I think it was a coalition government. Churchill was in charge but because the war was over everybody had to vote again for a new government and Labour got in. It was worse then than it was during the war, rations went right down. We couldn't get any coal and electricity wasn't going properly. They made such a mess of everything, that they've hardly been in since. People blamed the Labour Party at the time but when you look at it they had such a mess to clear up I suppose. They had to get things built. During the 1950s they started building.

Rationing went on until 1953 because when my daughter Christine was born in 1953 she had to have a ration book. I went in the shop one day with my ration book and said "I want a book of butter please" and the woman said "You can have as much butter as you like". I couldn't believe it. I went "what, rations gone?!" It just went all of a sudden, I couldn't get over it, couldn't believe it.

Ron was born in 1935 and Terry in 1938, so both were very young during the war.

Neither will say very much about the war, their memories blanked out by the loss of childhood.

Hilda's memories help to cast some light on their experiences.

# RON and TERRY

## blanking out

**RON:** I don't really remember the war. I went away. I think we went there by train and I had short trousers on. We went somewhere else first but I don't remember anything much. Then I got taken to a great big house with a matron. It was a big house with steps leading up to it.

I remember playing on the beach and all the crabs, massive great crabs. It was a private beach, belonging to the house. The nearest little town was Ashburton. It was a massive house with wide stairs. Very posh inside the house. Probably owned by some rich man. It was requisitioned for the war effort.

They marched you off to bed. I can remember the march we used to have to march to bed with this tune played on the piano. To get to school you had to walk down a country road.

You could see Plymouth in the distance and the search lights. It was a dock area. You used to see bombs in the distance. I can remember playing on the beach.

### Tearful times

One time I got a brush on the backside and I cried. On Christmas Day they took me before the matron cos I kicked up a load of noise during the night. I was hungry and I woke up from excitement, woke everybody up. There was a present on the end of everyone's bed, that parents had sent in. Mum and Dad had sent it in months before. I can't recollect it all now. I remember the country lanes in Devon.

Blank, my memory, altogether blank. Some old girls at 90 can go back to five years old. I can't understand it.

*HILDA: I think you're blanking it out, Ron. You told me you wet the bed and they gave you a cold shower as punishment.*

Yeah, I believe so. I was sort of lonely and all in the doldrums at that home. I felt lost. It was a different way of life, a strange time of life. We were all so separated during the war. But I survived it all.

### Coming home

I think I remember coming home to see Mum and Dad after being in the country all that time. I thought the house was really dirty and I didn't want to come home. I just had to accept it, I suppose.

I didn't like it at school cos the boys would take the rise. They knew all about us having a second hand shop. I can remember all that part clearly. It's the early part I can't remember.

I remember having fleas at school. Lice comb they used to use. Had to go to the clinic.

*Do you remember having your gas mask?*

I remember having a gas mask but I never used it. It goes over your head and it's black and brown. You never ever used them. They were just in case the Germans dropped a gas bomb, but they never did.

**Terry:** I remember sitting on the coastline and looking in the sea. There was different colour to a bit of the sea, like a greyish colour. I was asking an old seaman about it. "That's where it's deeper", he said.

I was an evacuee in a home during the war. You had your beds and there were beds on the other side, in two rows. One time I was looking through the window. The blinds were left open by mistake and you could see the search lights. I saw a plane caught up in the search lights and I was getting interested. Then along comes this woman and she closed the blinds down and I couldn't see anything.

I went to infants school. I was walking along the road and there were these American army trucks going by with great big stars on them. All the kids shouted out "Yankie, throw sweets out". They were throwing tons of sweets out. I got a Mars bar.

I don't remember Mum coming down to visit. There was some story about a train set but I don't know, I didn't get it.

When you went to bed you had to march with a kind of regimental tune on the piano. But maybe Ronnie told me that.

I was in a home on my own at first. I liked that but then I went to the second home where Ronnie was and they all said "That's your brother, Ronnie".

---

**You heard rumours that there was a war on. "A war, what's that?" we thought.**

---

They all said "There's a war going on." I didn't know anything. I asked my mum where babies come from. All she done was laugh. She never stopped laughing for ages. I thought "What's so funny about it?" She kept laughing and she wouldn't tell me. Ronnie told me all about it in the end.

I was playing up one day, got told to wait outside for the matron. I'm not sure what she done. I can't remember if she hit you with something, or what. I was only about five years old.

I remember once we went to the fields and I did it in my trousers. I had to run back. I remember that I thought "I'll get in a lot of trouble". But I don't think I did for some reason. I must have been in the good books that time.

### Coming home

I come home on the tube. You had to stop at Mile End station because it was as far as the trains went. Had to get a bus from Mile End to Stratford. I remember sitting on the side seat and my feet couldn't touch the ground.

*Private house converted to home for evacuated babies*

# THE WELCHES

In contrast to the Shinglers, the Welches of the war generation form a large clan of siblings and cousins who grew up together in Deptford. Grandad John Welch was born in 1873. He married Mary Ann Gard of Chelmsford in 1893. They had twelve children who between them produced 62 grandchildren, born between 1918 and 1961.

The various branches of the family spread out through South East London, usually through taking up the opportunity of a house on the cottage estates of Downham and Bellingham. They kept in touch with Deptford and especially with Granny Welch who was quoted in the local press in 1950 as saying "There is nothing like being a grandmother for keeping you happy and fit". At that time all her descendants, including 11 great grandchildren, lived within three miles of her home and it was said that she did her family visiting on foot every weekend. Certainly the eight of her grandchildren featured here remember her very fondly, though their memories of her husband are much harsher.

Many of the Welch boys worked at Surrey Docks and knew each other well until the docks closed in the 1970s. Since a chance meeting of two branches of the family through a Deptford History Group event in January 1994, the Welches have started to pull together again with a series of reunions and photo-swaps.

*Granny Welch (Mary Ann Gard)*

# The Welch family

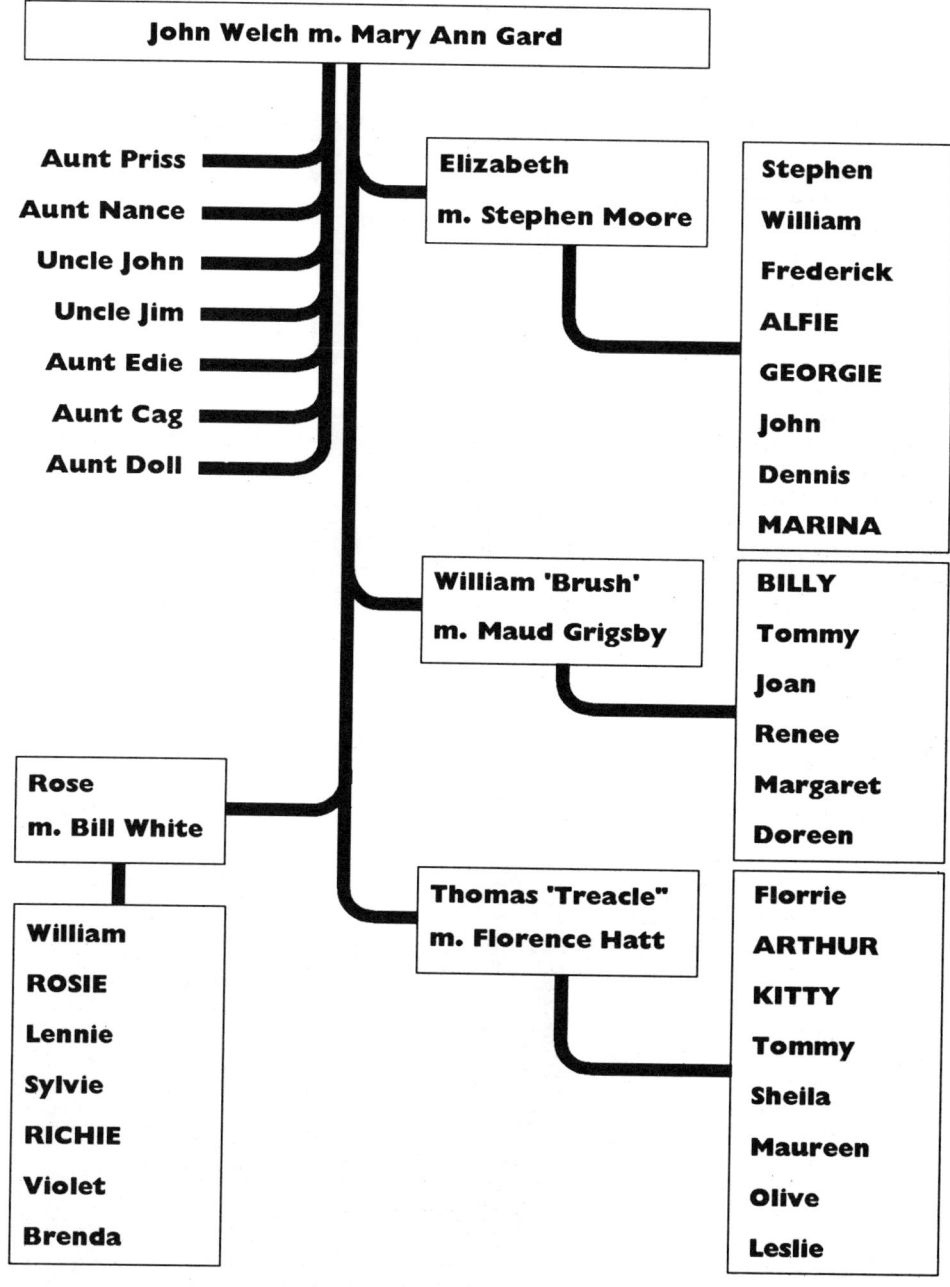

# ALF

## clearing the bloody battlefields

Alf was born in 1923 at Oareboro Road, Deptford, the fourth son of Elizabeth Welch and Stephen Moore. The family moved to Downham when he was three and then managed an off licence at Bell Green from 1937.

Alf joined up in August 1942, following his older brothers. With only basic first aid training he was drafted into the medical corps. His unit was the only hospital to serve on the front line and the effects of the job stayed with him for many years. The medics were kept in the hold of the troop ships and Alf remembers the terror of the depth charges exploding all around. The horror of watching a ship go down when hit was later outweighed by seeing men burn when tanks caught fire. There were some benefits to being a medic, however, including a certain respect from enemy troops.

When the unit was disbanded after the war Alf was sent to Mestre near Venice where he was the matron's driver in a hospital. There he met a young Italian maid and decided at once that he wanted to marry her. "I had some bad times in the army. In the medical Corps one sees the worst of war, in the field and in the wards. But I got a reward, a flower of Italy."

As a young boy I used to visit Granny Welch at 48 Blackhorse Road, Deptford. In that road we had quite a few uncles and aunts and grandmother Moore lived there as well. She used to have ladies in for a glass of gin, pinch of snuff and read the tea leaves for them.

Granny Welch was a much loved lady. Of a lunch time she would pop up to the Black Horse pub for a glass or two of mild ale and a chat to friends. During the week the women wore peak caps and their aprons were sacks which had been boiled and boiled until soft. But high days and holy days, they would have lovely felt hats with feathers or maybe flowers and artifical cherries.

I remember, when staying at Blackhorse Road, going across to the timber yard for a pennyworth of odd bits of wood. I always asked for a pennyworth of wood for 'Poll' as she was known. He would always give her more, pushing bits down hard into a sack. Other times I would go to the shop at the top of the road, a very dark shop lit by oil lamp. I'd take a basin for mustard or pickles or jam or oil and vinegar, at a penny a time. Fridays would always be fish, or jellied eels and mash.

I recall one time when a wedding or Christmas party was held in the middle of Blackhorse Road, with barrels of ale and tables of food. The party went on so late that the local police turned up. Made no difference, after a short while they joined in and were soon as drunk as all the others.

The best time of the year was August and September when all the Welch family, along with hundreds of Londoners, went hop picking. Up early each morning, take sandwiches or toast to the fields. Then on Saturday afternoon all the men would come down. This turned into a few drinks or more and sing-songs at the pub. On Sunday morning the men played Penny Up The Wall. This was tossing a penny each taking turn. The nearest to the wall took the lot. Sunday lunch time meant more drinking.

## The start of the war

Come the war years, we had moved from Downham to Bell Green. Brother Bill and Dad were managing this off-licence at the bottom of Sydenham Road in Southend Lane. The war started and my father tried with all his might to get the authorities to give him a machine gun. He said "I can see everything that's coming down from Crystal Palace and Forest Hill". He tried his utmost, thinking that was the ideal spot to have a machine gun.

I remember when the war broke out. We were sitting there listening to the radio that Dad made. That radio cost him £5 and it came in 40 pieces which Dad and I put together about six times, different pieces every Sunday, until eventually it worked.

Neville Chamberlain announced we were at war. The sirens sounded and we went down the shelter. Within three minutes the all-clear sounded. Nice sunny day, I believe.

## The shelter

We had an Anderson shelter down at the bottom of the garden. You could get six people in there, we usually had seven. We had bunks and we used to stay in there all night. The siren would go again at half past six in the morning. Dad didn't always come down. He used to stay in the house, and any of the boys that could stay in the house would, cos they didn't want to come down. All the old people knew that there was an underground street, running all the way round the gasworks. The whole thing used to get flooded but people still used to use it.

When Mum, Marina, Dennis, John, and George were evacuated down to Devon, my friend used to come and stay with us. I asked my father if he would take us both to the pub. One particular night we had drunk more than we ought to. We got back just before nine o'clock and went down the shelter. That was the Saturday night. On Sunday morning my friend got up, my father got up and they left me there. All the water was coming in the shelter. That was the morning they came back from Devon and I think if they hadn't come back I would have been drowned.

## Fear and fascination

When the others were evacuated, I worked in a grocers on Sydenham Road. I used to come home on my trade bicycle and my father would be at home in the off-licence. I was coming down Sydenham Road and the planes were coming down, dropping bombs all the way down the road. I got home to the off-licence but I couldn't get in, all the doors were locked. I tried the side door, Bang! Bang! Bang! Suddenly I got the door open, I went in and I noticed Dad under the kitchen sink. We had a shelter but he was in the kitchen cooking the dinner. I remember seeing old Dad there, under the kitchen sink. He was on his own and I was on the way home, what could I do? On a bicycle you think "Oh I can beat this" and you go tearing down the road. I think everybody was frightened of those first bombs.

GEORGIE: *I can remember coming home on leave for a weekend when the flying bombs had just started. Marina, Dennis, and John were at home and they were small youngsters. We heard the noise and they ran out the front to look. Well, me coming from the navy, I tried to drag them in and they looked at me as though I was around the bend! "What's the matter with him?" kind of thing.*

People at home grew up with the noise. You knew while you heard the noise you were safe, it was when it stopped that you were frightened wondering where it was going to drop. I'm fully convinced everybody was afraid when the bombs got close. Just before I got called up the air raids started. You would hear the air raids going on but you just carried on working. The shrapnel was the most frightening thing, more so than the bombs. It would be flying all over the place.

They bombed Surrey Docks in August 1940. It was on the Saturday afternoon they set fire to the place with the incendiaries, and then all through the night the bombers were coming over. They could see the fire so they knew exactly where they were going. At that time I don't think we were afraid of it but as things got closer there was some fear. Even in the armed forces people would put on a brave face but I know everyone I met during the war was afraid of getting killed in a foreign land and not coming home.

## Joining up

I was about 19 when I joined up. I spent very little time in this country. I went to Scotland for a few weeks, and then, thank goodness, I went overseas. I couldn't afford to stay, not on 14 shillings a week.

I joined up at a place called Fleet just outside Aldershot. There was a barracks there, a training centre. The sergeant told me what's expected of you. "Are you married?" No I weren't married. "Have you a mother?" Yes. So it was expected that you should send so much money home a week to your mother. Usually half your wages. So I sent seven shillings a week home to my mother.

So truly I couldn't afford to stay in this country. Going overseas cigarettes were more or less free all the time. Not only from the issue but from the people in this country. Schools used to send you out cigarettes. The children would get a collection so there'd be a note that this parcel came from such and such a school and they would expect you to write back. We got so many cigarettes, I was smoking maybe 80 a day. There was a story that the battle of Tunis was won on cigarettes and tea.

## Training

*How was it that you finished up in the medical corps?*

When I got called up after doing entry training, suddenly there was a need for more medical personnel. I had no qualifications. I didn't want to be a medic. But once you're there your conscience gets the better of you. You don't want to do it but you're trained. So I was in the Royal Army Medical Corps (RAMC). I thought it was Royal Army Machine Gun Corps - wishful thinking, never mind!

*What was the training ?*
A six weeks rushed course of first aid and everything else. The main thing was if someone stopped breathing, or to see which is the most serious case. I remember the sergeant saying: "If a man over there has got his hand hanging off and this man here has got blood squirting out all over the place, who do you treat first?" You treat the one with blood squirting out all over the place before the one with his hand damaged. That's the sort of training you had. You stop bleeding and cover everything up. That was all.

In the basic training, you got the mock-up wounds. They were very effective. The make-up on the face looked as though they was in a state of shock. They had a bone sticking out; it wasn't real, it was made up, but that prepared you for what you would see later on.

When I'd done entry training and medical corps training I went to Peebles near Edinburgh. There was a big hospital there and we were called to duty.

*When was the first occasion you met anybody that was ill?*
The first occasion after training, was in Scotland. Someone had collapsed on the pavement. I didn't really know what it was cos I was still only just past training. I smelt their breath. They were diabetic and they had collapsed in a coma. I had no sugar but someone had a boiled sweet, and that was that, it worked. That was very satisfying.

The next one was an epileptic fit. But the one after that was on New Year's Day, still in Peebles. My pal and I were detailed to pick up a corpse. We were driven to a remote croft by WVS ambulance. The soldier had been celebrating New Year and drunk too much whisky. We were putting him on the stretcher; my friend had the feet, I had the shoulders, and as I picked him up he exhaled all the air in his lungs. My mate got scared and run off, but eventually we got the body to the mortuary. When we got back the sergeant had kept our dinner warm but, although he hadn't died of any infectious disease whatsoever, before I could eat anything I wanted to wash and scrub my hands.

## Shipped out

We was the 76th general hospital. There was a sister unit. They should have gone before us but they had trouble so we went first. We left Peebles in the early hours of 3rd January 1943. All secret, but local people were out in force to see us off. We slid down the Clyde from Greenock on a cargo ship converted for troops called the *New Holland*. As a matter of interest, although I didn't know at the time, my brother Steve was coming up the Clyde on *HMS Mauritius* for repairs at Greenock. We passed each other not knowing.

We didn't know each other very well in the unit until we got on board the ship. That's when everybody got close together. It was about the best unit ever put out to sea. Apart from one man, everybody used to drink and everybody liked food. Even the colonel and sergeant-major had their drink. The CO would find us somewhere where you could get fresh vegetables and drinks, wherever we went.

There was six of us from South East London. Naturally we stuck together though none of us knew each other before that. We used to go into this canteen and they still had beer and stuff. It was a merchant ship and they still had all their supplies.

Not once in all that trip did I take my boots off. Not once.
*MARINA: No wonder your socks used to smell when you used to come home!*
We always had to be ready, whatever the situation. That took you out from other troops. You was expected to be there and be ready but the six of us made

sure that if it was going to happen we still had a good time. So I think we were drunk as newts mostly every night for two or three weeks. The padre asked who could play the mouth organ. I could and like a fool I said so. I puffed and sucked on this thing all the way to Algiers.

**Boats going down**

Once you see a ship going down it does scare you. Everybody gets frightened at sometime or other. The scary part was when there was attacks on the convoy, these navy ships going around with depth charges. We were down in the hold and the noise of those depth charges exploding down there was very scary. We couldn't always tell what they were doing so we didn't know what was going on. If you are below the water level when they explode, it's frightening cos you've got the hollow of the ship, the metal of the ship, the water and the noise going across.

It's bad enough when you are on land, but when you're at sea, its very, very frightening. I couldn't swim. Afterwards I learned it's far better not to be able to swim, cos then you're not struggling all the time. There was nowhere you could swim to or float to anyway.

In the army you had these padded life jackets. It was only canvas. Once it got wet, it would have taken you down. It could only save you for a couple of hours and that would be it.

This whole thing at sea was very scary. You imagine a ship with thousands of troops on it and what would happen if it got hit. We were down in the hold, the idea being that if it got hit and it didn't sink, the medics could attend to people that were injured up above. But you didn't stand a chance down there, no way would you have got out at all.

GEORGIE: *In cases where they had to close those watertight doors, if you were in there, whether you were alive or not, if orders came to close watertight doors, you closed the doors. Those people in there would perish, purely to save the rest of the crew and the ship.*

Twelve days at sea - rough sea - we were all sick as dogs. Landing at Algiers, the unit moved off and us six Londoners were detailed to help unload the equipment, all the time being bombed and blasted. That took two days. We were sitting in dock and there was nothing you could do, with the bombing all around you. It was frightening. When people say they weren't frightened, the youngsters may not be frightened, because in their innocence they know less, but I've yet to find a person when coming to a situation like that, that weren't scared.

Then our unit was in transit over the tops of the mountains above Algiers. The first night there, me and two regular army Scotsmen dodged out down a goat path to a little hamlet and got as drunk as newts on local wine. Leaving the bar, we didn't know which way to turn and we finished up in the Casbah for two days. When we got back to unit I got my first charge, not for being drunk and absent but for mixing with old soldiers and their drinking habits.

It was the rainy season. The first task for the hospital was helping out another unit in three inches of mud. We were glad to move on and set up our own site. From there we moved to lots of different sites, then to the plains outside the town of Tunis. As we advanced to Tunis we were stopped by a large group of Germans. We were showing the Red Cross and they fired above our heads. We set up a hospital unit next to a German hospital. During the night a strong wind blew up and down came all our hospital tents. Tunis is a flat salt bed with about three inches of soil and our wooden pegs were useless but the Germans came to our help with steel pegs.

You were issued with a high density silk triangle. It was bright yellow, like a parachute style. So if the planes come over not knowing how far you'd advanced, you pulled out these things, on mass wherever you were, maybe 10 of you or 20 of you, and the planes were supposed to know you were British or Allied forces. They said that always worked but I know one of our cousins' battalion got in serious trouble. They'd advanced so much the Allies didn't know they were there. They pulled these things out but some of the Allies didn't realise what that meant! So it didn't always work.

## Patching up the horrors

I've seen people burning. You've seen these things on the television or films. If a spitfire or a bomber comes down in flames, they can parachute out. But if a tank gets hit with a shell, and catches on fire, there's very few can get out of that.
*Would they arrive at your hospital base?*
I wasn't necessarily in a hospital base. The hospital I was in was the only British hospital serving the front line. I've got a clasp to say that I served in the front line. If a tank was seen, you've got shells coming over but you've got to go and get the people. That is frightening, not only the thought of those people there, but you've got to go there as well, to collect them.

The troops used to sleep underneath the tanks which was against all the rules, because if it was the rainy season then the tanks would sink down into the mud. This fella had slept outside and the tank had sunk down onto his foot. His ankle was coming off. My friend managed to take his foot off. I suppose that was the result of training. He could do it, and whether I could have done it I don't know. That was the first bloody operation, I suppose.

Mind you, in Africa I think we was very lucky with the enemy we were fighting. With the Italians and the German Wermacht there were very few of the SS there. The German army recognised Red Cross. So you was pretty safe to go out with your Red Cross, unless you were in the middle of it, where they were shooting at each other. In general, you could go ahead and there was no fear of being captured. Because if you was captured you still done the same work as what you were doing before.
*So that's quite different from other members of the army?*
Oh yes, it was quite unique. If you was captured then you had to work in an Italian or German hospital, or vice versa. We had Germans and Italians working with us.

## Goes with the job

The job in the Medical Corps did effect me. When I was at Casserta we took over a prisoner of war hospital. It was a German hospital with British prisoners. I got on well enough with the Austrians and the Germans. There was one fella there, an Italian lieutenant. He had a kidney removed and that was a big thing in those days. It was a British officer who had done the operation. I was on duty that night. It was one or two in the morning and he was really ill. I got on to these two Austrian orderlies about him and they said, "Well he's been like that for some time". Then I went up to get the German doctors, but they wouldn't come down. I was quite shaken. I went to the other part of the hospital where there was a nursing sister on duty. She said, "You go and tell them, if they don't come down there'll be serious trouble". So I got them down and they asked me to get a certain drug. You had to have sterilised water though, and there was no water. So I tried to use something else...and he died.

Years later, in 1952, I suddenly went a bit unstable. I don't know what it was, I felt it was my fault that he had died. It might have been a build up of other things I had seen. What used to get to me was the youngsters coming in in such a state, their lives finished. They were shelled or had shrapnel in their spine or heads, and there were just like little children afterwards. It was the build up of all that and that was the last straw. I went to the chemists and got these tablets. The next few years I was on drugs and everything. My doctor said I might have to see a psychiatrist. Anyhow, he gets talking to me. He said "You shouldn't worry about this, it happens to us all in the medicine profession". How doctors live without being effected I don't know.

## Off to Italy

War in Africa ended and it took us five days to get from Bizerta in North Africa across to Taranto in Italy which should take less than a day. There was a storm in the Medi-terranean. When we got to Taranto that's when the Italian Navy sunk all their ships. We stayed two days and then went up to Bari, Biseglic then Trani. We stayed at Trani for some time but then the unit was disbanded, the most famous general hospital serving in Africa, awarded the Africa Star on 14th December 1943 with Clasp 1 First Army. They brought people out from England to replace us. We were sent round to the Far East and then I went to so many places.

## Meeting up

GEORGIE: *What about when you met Georgie Spooner?...Now their mother is another sister. My mother was the eldest, and auntie Priss was the next eldest, and she married a Spooner.*

Georgie Spooner was in the army. I used to write to granny Welch, quite regularly and she would always say "Georgie Spooner is in Africa. You should meet up with him." We did get close to each other and we tried to get in touch but it seems one day you get close and the next you're somewhere else. He was in tank recovery. He would collect tanks that were damaged, and try and get them back before the Germans came. He was as mobile as what we were in my unit.

It went on and on. In Naples I was in bed, it was about 10 o'clock and suddenly someone breaks in the building. It was a cousin, it wasn't George, it was Lennie, his brother in the navy. I said "What are you doing here?" "Oh, I've come to take you out. We're going down the pub."
"I'm not allowed out now. I'm not allowed out until five o'clock this evening."
"No, it's alright, I've been to see the sergeant major. As long as you report on tonight, it's alright."

We went down to Naples. There was Prince Umberto's palace there, taken over by the forces, and in the gatelodge they had made a sort of pub, called the St George. Anyway Georgie Spooner's there and, of course, the place was full of Deptfordites. We was ordering 16 pints at a time. The Town Major was a British officer and he insisted on British licence laws being kept, so they had to close at 3 o'clock. All the bars outside were closed at three o'clock as well. We worked around it. Georgie says "We'll go round the local bar" and although it was closed and the shutters were down he managed to get the drinks. I don't know how many days we went on like that. I was glad when he went back!

## An Italian marriage

When the war finished I got sent to Naples where there was a big fascist population and they were expecting trouble. So all troops were confined to barracks except military police. Nothing happened but that unit was the worse place I've ever been. The sergeant major didn't drink and the colonel didn't drink.

Then I went to Venice. When I got there the sergeant major said, "Well, what do you want to do?" He said, "Do me a favour, go down to the sister's mess. You won't need to do anything but sit and talk. It's a nice big villa, a mile away from the hospital...all girls." It was a real luxury, waited on hand and foot. We had German cooks in the kitchen, Polish guards, and I was in charge. I became the matron's driver, took her to the hospital in the morning, picked her up later, and the rest of the day was mine.

That's where I met my wife. She was working there as a maid. I was sitting in the kitchen and she walked in, the most beautiful young girl I had ever seen. She had flashing eyes, by that I mean eyes that moved from one side to the other due to an inherited muscle thing. At

50

that moment I said to myself "I am going to marry this girl" and I fought all objections. I had a lovely time there, didn't want to come home.

Her sister, Elvira, also worked there. Before I was introduced to my wife I used to sit out in the garden. Elvira would be there, maybe shelling peas, and we would sit and talk.

By the time it came to courting my wife, she wouldn't come out into the town or anywhere with me because they were afraid in those days of having their hair cut off by the local people for mixing with the foreign troops, whether it was English, French, Polish or American, whatever. So I couldn't go out with my wife without an escort. There was still that old-fashioned thing of a chaperone. Her sister was older so I could take her out, but there was nothing to that! Still, Elvira was a lovely girl. Being in the ambulance was very good. I was getting the best treatment.

GEORGIE: *I was away fighting the war while that was going on!*
MARINA: *We were at home starving!*

*What was the family's reaction when you started going out with their younger one?*

They didn't know. Lidia's mother and father died when she was six but her brother was very strict. She said "how can I tell my brother" but I said "you're 21, he can't stop you from getting married" so she plucked up the courage and told them that she wanted to see me. I went around there and it was all fine.

They had a very hard life. It was all girls and one brother. Part of the farm should have gone to the family but the brother didn't want it so his cousin got it. The two eldest sisters had left home and he got called up in the forces. They had to struggle all the time, these younger girls, on their own.

When I got married he said "I've got nothing to give you", because they're very strict about dowries usually. I didn't expect anything, we don't here. Anyhow a few years later when my young sister-in-law got married and Elvira got married, there was argument about their dowry, so my brother-in-law said, "I've got nothing. I've got a table, that's all I've got from the family" and he said to each husband, "You can have a leg and when Alf comes over he can have a leg, and that will leave me a leg".

*There wasn't any feeling of enmity on either side?*

My mother didn't like it at first and she and my wife didn't get on well for quite some time. It wasn't the fact that she was Italian, it was the fact that someone had taken away her son. After about two years they got on great.

*Did you learn Italian?*

I did learn some Italian, enough to get by and to cope with restaurants. It all depends which part of Italy you come from because the dialect is so strong. I learnt Italian in Naples. A lot of that is hand and facial language. When I got to Venice I couldn't make myself understood, it was very difficult. Then I learnt the dialect. I suppose the best Italian I speak is Milanese. I could understand them more than any other Italian dialect. It's not only the dialect, it's the tone. Its a very musical language. Even now we have certain problems. When Lydia's saying a certain thing, it's a tone she uses, and even now I take it the wrong way. It's the same when she hears me or my son speaking English. Only a fortnight ago she misunderstood what he was saying, she was very upset. I said "Well, you misunderstood him".

## Dealing with the end of war

Everybody was just getting by. There was all sorts of scams, like army blankets being made into coats by the local people. There was a huge army lorry on the island just outside Venice and no-one knew what to do with it. It cost too much to bring back here so what do they do? No end of them used to disappear overnight. No-one took much notice of it. Some of them sold them. One of my mates, an ambulance driver, went missing for months. When they found him, he had no ambulance. He had sold it, but he said it got pinched and that he had been out looking for it!

This is what went on. The war had finished. Even the German prisoners we had working for us in the hospital would disappear overnight. They were dividing up Berlin then, and they would think "My family's in the Russian zone" and they wanted to get there to get them out. This was the feeling. I knew full well what was going and what food was missing from the kitchen. They was building up a little supply for one night when they're going to go off. They was hurting nobody.

GEORGIE: *That was the wisest thing. The authorities had to look after the running of public utilities and in Germany imagine that. They're not going to bother about troops that don't want to stay there, which they've got to disperse anyway. So if they do go, they're doing everyone a favour.*

Plus bearing in mind in the medical corps, what could we do about it? We can't shoot them. It was going on a large scale, it wasn't just a local thing. Why should I interfere with a bloke who is trying to get back to his family?

## Coming home

I came on my first leave from Italy in October 1945. I got to Peterborough on a Lancaster Bomber, sitting on the deck in a tiny little space. How these things got into the air at all is a marvel. It took me eight hours from Naples to Peterborough but from Peterborough to London, it took 12 hours by train. I was looking forward to an English autumn but after 28 days I was due back and for weeks I couldn't get here because of the fogs. When I got demobbed, I was happy to be here, but now I wish I'd gotten demobbed in Italy. The biggest mistake I ever made was coming back here.

I would have stayed if I had somewhere to live there. My wife wanted to come here to meet the family but now I want to go back, she wants to stay. Looking back, I think the way of life and what's happening to this country now...In Italy, it's a closer way of life, a more touching, friendly way of life. I would have had a happier life if I'd stayed there.

I was glad to get back to England at that time. Coming back here after the European thing.... We weren't all that bad off, but we didn't get the aid that we should have been getting. When I saw the aid that was going into Germany I think we was sent down the drain by the USA. But it don't matter what government got in, I don't think there's much anybody could have done.

*What did London look like when you got back from the war?*

It looked very nice to me apart from the bomb damage. I think we've been very backward in coming forward to rebuild London with the opportunity there was to renovate the buildings that we had left and smarten them up. We were very lax in doing that. Shortages in material and everything else after the war. You couldn't even get a pack of nails. You had to search everywhere for tin tacks for furniture. We were in debt to the USA. If you looked at London there was so much damage done, but it was still nice to come back to, though I wish I had come back with money to spend.

# GEORGE
## eager for the sea

George was the fifth son of Elizabeth Welch and Stephen Moore. He was evacuated in the first wave to Devon with his mother, two younger brothers and baby sister Marina, but they soon returned because Mum was worried about "the boys at home".

Always desperate to go to sea, George sneaked off to shipping offices whenever he could and eventually got a place on a Dutch coaster...without telling his family.

After a severe accident in a hydraulic lift, George joined the Royal Navy at the age of 17. A narrow escape in the North Sea was followed by the long haul to Australia where he awaited further orders. By the time he was drafted onto a battle ship the Japanese war was over and the ship toured the area on a variety of missions from trouble-shooting in Tokyo to collecting the Governor General from Tasmania.

Because of his early service in the Merchant Navy, George was demobbed at 21 rather than the usual 25.

There are seven boys in the family. Steve and Bill have passed on. Steve was in the Royal Navy and Bill was in the Army. Then came Fred who was in the army from the first. He was in the Territorials. He got called up before the war actually started, then he was sent home. Of course then it came along and he was called up again. There's Alf who went into the Medical Corps and me who went into the Royal Navy. Then there was John, who eventually went into the army, and Dennis who went into the army for a short time. Sister Marina, the youngest of us, stayed at home, and did nothing for the war effort whatsoever. So that's us.

My father was a dabbler in antiques. He was a professional French polisher, furniture restorer and antique manufacturer. Mum, having eight children, was just a housewife. She was born in 1895; Dad was a year older. He came from Bethnal Green, somewhere in that area, across the water.

## Dad's leg

Dad had a wooden leg. He lost his leg when he was 12. He fell down and grazed his knee. His mother, Granny Moore, who I always considered an old witch cos she made medicines and potions and took part in telling fortunes and drinking gin and pinching snuff, used one of her treatments and he never got better. He had to go to Mildmay Hospital, up near Balls Pond Road, but it was too late. It gradually got shorter and shorter.

I suppose it was gangrene. I think he had about six operations. He had pieces cut off each time until there was a very short piece left. Didn't stop him from cycling or playing football though. He could carry us on his shoulders as well. That's after he had a few pints.

He got an artificial leg from Roehampton hospital, a cork one. His mother had to find 24 people who promised to donate a guinea. I've got the certificate that eventually got him an artificial leg. Now that must have been when he was young, but as he got older he grew out of it. At one time he had this artificial leg that he couldn't get on with at all so he made his own, which was more like a stump. There was a leather top part with a socket, the knee part was a leather strap and the leg went down to a three inch stump at the bottom. The old artificial leg was laying about for years apparently. One time when Monday came along, the wash day, Mum used his artificial leg to boil the washing in the copper in the corner of the scullery. When they moved house Dad suddenly said: "What happened to that leg of mine?" and Mum said: "Well, it must have got lost in the move". So for years he was still using this leg he made himself. He wore that until he died.

*MARINA: Dennis and John tried sawing the ends off when he was asleep one Christmas. They used toy saws or something. He woke up too quickly but he had that saw mark in it afterwards!*

It never worried him at all, it never bothered him. He just got on with his life.

*ALFIE: He was called up to the army in the first war. He was called up on one day and discharged the next day, as unfit. And he never received a pension!*

*MARINA: No, he got a shilling, he had a day's pay.*

*ALFIE: I think it was the sergeant who noticed that he'd only got one leg. I think his elder brother must have dragged him into joining up. He was very strict, Uncle Jack. He was a tough sergeant major, a big bully. I thought my father was strict. At my father's table you daren't take your eyes off your plate. If you looked at your brother's plate that was it! But Uncle Jack! We had to go there for Sunday dinner. He treated us the same as he treated his sons and his daughter. They had the old cane and when he was finished they automatically had to get up and clear the tables. He was always criticising the food, destroying the mother's cooking.*

## Evacuation

Things seemed to roll on until school broke up and we got evacuated down to

Exeter. There was myself, John, Dennis and Marina as a baby. Because there was four of us and mother we couldn't get placed in any ordinary home. In the end Mrs Rowe, who was organising all the evacuees being placed, said "Oh well, you will have to come home with me". We went to her house which was rather good actually. She used to employ gardeners, maid, chauffeur, cook. We had huge meals and we thought we were the king pins. Taken to school by the chauffeur every day! We didn't realise how lucky we were. We came home after a matter of weeks because Mum was worried about the boys at home.

## Slipping away to sea

Anyway we came home and I got various jobs, here and there. Then I started going up to the shipping offices in the City, trying to look for a ship. Without Mum's knowledge, obviously. I was straight out of school and she didn't want me to go she already had the other four gone. I was always writing off to ships. Apparently every time a letter came home, Mum just used to burn it.

I went up there for about six months. I was doing three days work to get sufficient money so Mum had the impression that I was at work. I used to go down to Catford and get a 47 bus up to the City to go around shipping offices. I got to know them quite well, or they got to know me. The merchant seamen were coming in, signing onto ships and signing off of ships. I was asking over the counter if there was any vacancies for ships. My green attitude. I went to Dock Street, Swedish Lines, every office I could find, but they didn't want to know.

In the end I got into the Dutch shipping office. They seemed very friendly. One day there was a seaman there talking to the chap behind the counter. He said: "Go on, let him have a go" and the chap behind the counter said: "Do you want this job as a galley boy?" I jumped at it so he sent me to the medical officer and other offices to get clearance. Once I'd done that he gave me a warrant to be at Hull the next morning. I went home and packed a kit bag that one of the brothers had left at home. Our house had a long path around the back that came out at a gate down the very end. So I slipped out. I was about 16 then. I left Mum a note "It's all right Mum. I've gone to sea. It's only a coaster."

I had to get authority to go on this ship so I got my mate Ginger to come along. We went up to the station, King's Cross or Liverpool Street, whichever goes to Hull. Ginger saw me off, very late at night, and I got to Hull about 6am. I went into a cafe and then I had to find King George V Dock. I remember going down to these docks and there was the ship and this blooming big ladder. I went to an officer's cabin and he said "Who are you, what are you?" I said "I'm the new galley boy" and gave him my papers. He took me to the galley and then the chief steward took me to a cabin and said "There's your bunk". It was rather a nice cabin actually, because it was a ship that used to take a few passengers, pre-war, and this was a two-berth cabin on the upper deck. He said "Get your working clothes on and go up and see the cook and you can start work".

I must admit I got in that cabin after they had let me off from work and I sat down and wondered what I had done, "What have I let myself in for?" I didn't have the nerve to run off the ship. If I'd had the nerve, I would have done.

The next morning the chief cook put me into the routine. Go down the end of the ship, down to the poop deck that's where all the potatoes are kept. At that stage, there were very few on board so there were only a few potatoes to peel.

After a fortnight they had to fumigate the ship. The rest of the crew took me on shore to a pub, a real sailor's den but they looked after me.

Once we went out to sea with the full crew I had to go down to the poop deck at six o'clock in the morning, pick up a hundredweight of potatoes, climb all the way back up the ladders, down the ladders, across the deck, up the ladder, down there, cross the deck. I had to peel this hundredweight of potatoes before eight o'clock. After six months of that I was an expert on potato peeling.

*ALFIE: And he has never peeled a potato for 45 years!*

I didn't see Mum and Dad until I got leave after about a fortnight. I went home for a couple of days at least. I got the impression Dad was as proud as punch. They told me I sent Mum grey and I can remember them all shouting at me. I didn't send her grey, I sent her a shilling a day, my pay. At that time Steve was away, Bill was away, Fred was away, and Alf was going away. So its a toss up who sent her grey. I can only put it down to Hitler's fault.

## Watching the boats go down

There was an occasion when I was in the Merchant Navy, when we were going down to West Africa, just past Gibraltar. There was a warning on board ship, the subs were about. We were in a convoy with about 75 ships, with four Royal Navy destroyers. In the middle of the night a torpedo sunk this oil tanker just across the way and before it actually sunk I could see the chaps on there lowering the lifefloat, which was just a coupling that went down a couple of runners into the sea, and they jumped out. I am sure that just before that torpedo struck it, they were off that ship, and on that float. It just burst into flames, obviously. My knees started knocking there, I couldn't stop them. I don't know if they survived. We just went on, we couldn't stop, this is the whole thing with convoys.

In all my time, the only lifebelt I had was like a rubber tyre. You blew it up to size and it had a distinguishing light, just a little red torch battery light, stuck on the side. You get a pitch black night and the waves coming over and all the rest, no one would see that little light. That was issued by the merchant service.

## Disaster in the lift

When we came back to Hull I signed off that ship. That was the only trip I did in the Merchant Navy because I couldn't get another ship. I decided to get a job up town so I could go round the shipping offices in the lunch-time. I got a job in a paper warehouse opposite the Old Bailey. Before I started I had to go and see the foreman in the basement warehouse who showed me how to work the hydraulic lift. You pulled the rope and up you went to street level. Next morning the foreman wasn't in but the manager said, "Go down and open the warehouse". So I went down, got on the hydraulic lift, and pulled the rope to go up. As you went up you were supposed to unbolt two flaps, push them up as you were going up and lower them into the street. But I didn't undo them and I got squashed in that lift. When I woke up I was in Bart's Hospital. Apparently my shoes got caught somewhere along the line and stopped the lift going completely up and saved me somewhat. I was unconscious in hospital for 36 hours, I think. I don't remember too much of that period

*ALFIE: I was home on leave at the time but due to go back the next day. Fred come home on compassionate leave, then Bill. I sent a telegram asking for compassionate leave but the answer was no. I took several days AWOL.*

*MARINA: Mum said when she went to see George he was just black. She was getting worried because he was beginning to swell. Then he got over that and Mum thought "That's good he's home again" but he went and joined the Royal Navy.*

## Joining up

I went down to Ennersdale Road and volunteered. I was $17\frac{1}{2}$ then. I went to Portsmouth for my training and then got put on a ship in Belfast. It was one of those old ones that the Americans supposedly gave us for bases. They gave us 50 of them soon after the beginning of the war and I think we had to give them bases in the West Indies or around that area. They were old ships. My one had a gun made by the American Radiator Company in 1917.

I was a seaman then, although they still tried to make me peel the spuds. I got the job as flunky for the first officer and a couple of other officers, which was damn good. There was a navigating officer and a Canadian Lieutenant. They got an allowance in their money to pay their flunky. It was about five bob a month or something like, but it was damn good. All you had to do was tidy up their cabin and make their bunk and that was it. The Canadian officer got packets of cigarettes each month from Canada and he used to give them to me.

I enjoyed that but I got so good that the captain ordered me to be his flunky and I never got a penny off him. I lost that job though. When you go into or out of the harbour you have to batten everything down. I had to batten down his cabin and tie up the bottles and things like that, making sure nothing moved. One day coming out I forgot to batten down and so when he came off the bridge after leaving harbour, his cabin was in a mess. He said, "You don't like this job do you?" and, after having such a cushy one before and getting paid for it as well, I said "No". So I did eventually lose that job.

### Stuck in the mines

I don't know how long we were on that ship. We were in the North Sea and we went into a mine field. Now how we got there is anyone's guess. Of course, me being an AB [able seaman], I wouldn't know, they wouldn't trust me! It struck exactly at 4 o'clock in the morning just as the watch was changing over. The majority of the ship's crew were wide awake. We had to go onto the fo'csle because the whole ship broke in half. We lost one man in that. There were some wounded that were on the after gun, where the mine had struck the propellers.

We couldn't get out. It was only off of Aberdeen, it wasn't far out but it was far enough if you couldn't swim. No-one could come and get us off, you see, because of the mines. Someone came out to try to rescue us and they got a cable across but it snapped. Eventually a Scottish fishing vessel came in and being timber hulled there was less chance of magnetic mines catching it. We had to jump on that and we eventually got ashore.

We had our survivors' leave and then we went back to barracks. I got pushed on a gunnery course in Whale Island, down at Portsmouth. It was considered to be the strictest gunnery school in the world at one time.

### The other side of the world

Soon after that I got a draft to Australia so that we would be there for when we were needed. I went out there on a passenger ship The *Aquitania*, which was a holiday for me. When you go on a troop ship you get your lifeboat stations and when you are lined up there you get your duties handed out. Another matelot [Royal Navy seaman of no rank] and myself didn't go to lifeboat stations. Whether we did that intentionally or not, I don't know. Maybe we were just somewhere else at the time. But it meant we didn't get any duties. So we had about five weeks getting to Australia without having to do any work.

We went to a navy camp in Sydney called 'The Golden Hind'. From there they would draw you onto any ships that needed their crew completing or renewing. I got drafted onto *HMS Anson* which was a big battle ship. I didn't like to go onto the battle ships. They were so strict in comparison with a destroyer. But anyway, I went and it turned out to best the best time I've had. So I was instinctively lucky there.

### Cruising after the war

The Japanese war had ended by that time, so again I was lucky. We just toured around. The ship had to go to Tasmania to pick up the Governor General of Australia, the Duke and Duchess of Gloucester and their children. That was a nice trip, going up the river into Hobart.

We came back and eventually we went up to Japan, into Tokyo and places like that, showing the flag mainly. When we were in Tokyo, Yokohama Bay, we had to go ashore as shore patrol to see that everything was in order when a navy boat came in. A group of us was picked to go ashore each night. The Yanks were in Tokyo with all these jeeps.

One night we went ashore and we were in a Japanese police station. There was one white Yank, one black Yank and a matelot. We got called out to a spot in Yokohama where there was some trouble. Another jeep was in front with another matelot, a black chap. We were chasing him and landed up in a crowded area.

The matelot in the jeep in front jumped out and went into this dark alleyway. Now this is in Japan, all bombed, and with these little wooden huts. I just stood there with the other two. Apparently one of these two Japanese had shot someone in a fight and this matelot was running after the chap who's got the gun. And all he's got, same as I had, is a truncheon!

Anyway, that all ended up well. We took this wounded Japanese person into the hospital which was just a hut. The chap in command of our jeep, the white Yank, said to me: "You stand outside and don't let anyone in this hospital." So I'm standing outside, stopping all these hundreds of Japs, but they all said or indicated that they were relatives. So I said "Alright then, you go in". They all put their shoes outside. The white Yank, the sergeant if he was a sergeant, calls out "What are you letting them all in for?" I said, "They're all his relatives". And at the front of the bungalow hospital there was all these shoes!

*Did you have much to do with the Japanese?*

No, not really. We just walked about as we would in any country. Being Jack Tar no one could make us frightened.

## Demobbed

I was demobbed before I was 21 because I had served in the Merchant Navy at 16 and they accounted that time onto my demob number. So I was demobbed with men who were much older.

## Romance

*Did you meet your wife during the war?*

No, after.

*Not much chance for romantic involvements in the navy?*

Oh, none at all! *[laughing]*. Well, when you called in at a port, you know you had to look around the town and....I know that I could have settled down iin various places.

## Post-war Politics

I think the government in 1946 was the most wicked of any we've ever had. I know we were short of everything and the Yanks had taken every penny we'd got before they gave us a slice of bread. I know we were broke but what they did then made us broker by nationalising everything.

*ALFIE: I can't see what any government could have done. We had strict rationing and you got your entitlement within the rationing, whereas if you went across the channel you was lucky if you got anything at all. By the time you got to the end of the queue there was nothing there.*

Yes, but at times there was nothing here for us with ration books. Let's be fair. When did you get an egg on a ration book?

*ALFIE: If there was eggs in, then you got eggs. You know full well your book was marked for eggs. And if you'd had eggs you couldn't get them again, until other people had had their eggs.*

Yes, but when were they in? In the end we had to rely upon Poland, that had been knocked about far worse than us, I would imagine. We were buying eggs from Poland, weren't we ?

*MARINA: We were worse off, after the war, for rations.*

*ALFIE: I'm comparing this country to how it was in Europe. They were very lucky if they got anything. Whether it was the corruption or not, I don't know. There certainly was a hell of a lot of corruption. Corruption is the war.*

*Before the election in '45, were you opposed to the Labour government?*

No, no. I wasn't opposed to them, although I had been brought up under politics. I used to listen to a communist and a conservative, arguing nightly. So I knew a bit about Harry Pollitt and 'Churchill the warmonger'. These are the expressions that they used. I remember being in the pub and I saw Churchill come past, doing an election thing. I heard a lot of people booing him. But I went back to me beer, having been brought up hearing that Churchill was a warmonger. I wasn't very strong on politics, although I suppose if anything, I was on the side of Labour, because my eldest brother was a strong 'leftie'. You take notice of your oldest brother.

That government did nothing for the troops that came home. They had gotten in because of the Beveridge thing, which promised everything, but they couldn't afford to buy it. In doing it on the cheap like they did, having to borrow such a great deal they let everyone down. Possibly they would have done differently if they had done it step by step, when it could be afforded. Then everything could have been worked out on a safer bet. But I think that was the worst government this country has ever had. The way the troops were treated. What did the prisoners of war in Japan get? Think of that.

DICKIE: *No matter what government has been in power since the war, nobody has ever done anything about it. Nobody has said, "Right we get in touch with Japan and demand it". They just let it slide.*

But that was the time when Churchill could have stood up, and it's a great shame. Now Churchill was the right man for the moment. He was a downright Conservative, but he could have stood up then, if he had been in power and wheedled his way, got things in, whereas old Clem Attlee was a kind-hearted man but his policies were wrong.

They should have admitted that we couldn't really afford the Beveridge plan straight after the war. But we went to America, got this loan, which was selling the crown jewels. We've sold them several times since, I know. In my heart, they let us down completely.

# MARINA
## sister of the seven gods

Marina was born in 1939 at Bell Green above an off-licence run by her parents, Stephen Moore and Elizabeth Welch.

The area was a target for bombers because of the gasworks. Bottles would be knocked off the shelf, and the family sometimes took the opportunity for a party by drinking what wasn't broken yet and throwing the bottles on the floor.

Although Marina's memories of the war itself are inevitably dim, she had seven older brothers who all served in the forces. Marina grew up with "these seven gods: my mum would say 'I've got seven boys' – she never mentioned me. Mum loved Mondays cos that was washing day. She'd wash, bleach, blue their shirts, on and on."

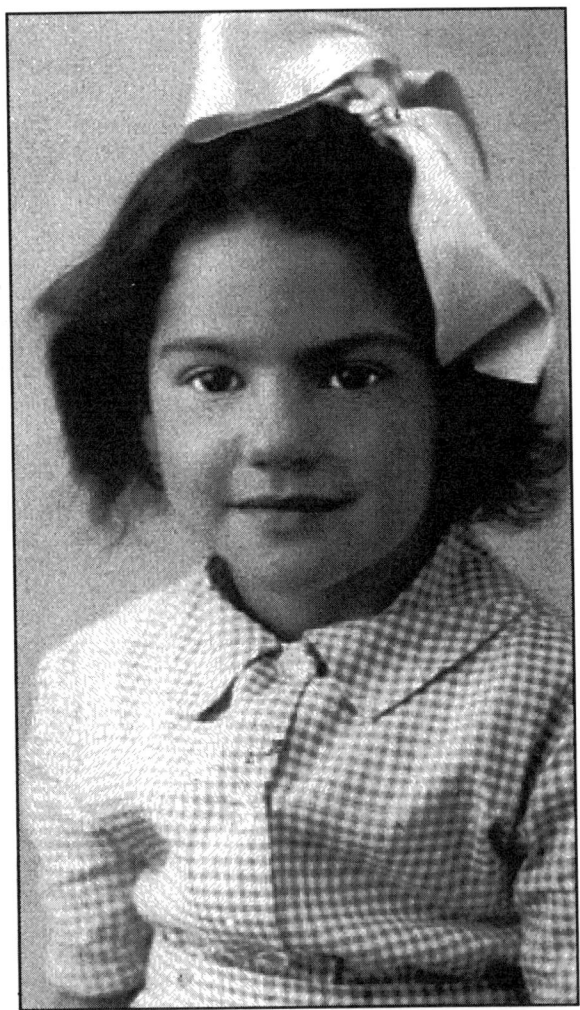

Certain things stick in my mind. Probably I remember things because I have been told them over and over again. When I was born my eldest brother was already in the Navy. He was 21 and married. My brother Fred was already in the Army, so that left five brothers at home. Three more went into the forces so that just left John, Dennis and me at home with Mum and Dad.

## The Start of the war

I remember the boys joining up. The first air raid they had that September, they all went down to the shelter in the garden and forgot they had me and left me in the house. That was September 3rd, the Sunday war was declared on Deptford Park. It was a false alarm.

At the beginning of the war, we were evacuated – George, John, Dennis, me and Mum. We went to Devon but Mum didn't like being away from the rest of the family, so we only stayed two weeks. We came back home because she worried about the boys that were just going or getting home on leave. She was so proud of all her boys. There was no-one in the world like her boys, so it was always a lot of tears when they were going and excitement when they came home. To me, there always seemed to be parties and celebrating someone coming home. There was always somebody or other, especially Fred, because he used to come home nearly every weekend. He was only stationed on the east coast on a gun. Whenever he came home the first thing he did as he came in the door would be to tip his kit bag out for us to rummage through. We'd find pencils, chocolate, smelly socks. I think he had the most smelly feet out of the whole family but we didn't get put off, we'd eat the chocolate. It was a real luxury.

I suppose because he was home every weekend, I knew Fred better than most of the others. He met his wife, Stella, on the gun site and they got married in October 1944. He was always sending telegrams home that he was getting married so they didn't believe him. He rushed home and said "Well, didn't you go to the registry office and book it?" It was a mad panic then. My dad was at work during the wedding!

We didn't know what Stella looked like. She arrived the day before and Fred wasn't home yet. She brought her friend, a woman sergeant who was absolutely enormous! I remember my mum being so worried, because she didn't know which one it was and didn't like to ask! We always helped them clean their buttons, and boots and things. We slid the buttons on this brass plate with a slit down the middle, to clean them without the polish getting onto their uniforms. I got quite good at cleaning boots, spit and polish.

*Was there talk of you evacuating again?*

No, my mum wouldn't go. She said that down in Devon she wasn't getting any news of the boys so she worried about them. If they came home, she wanted to see them. My dad was up here and she worried about him. She was happier among all the bombs, knowing she was there if the boys needed her.

Mum wrote to all five of the boys every day. She used to write quickly in the mornings, so that whoever was going to school could post the letters on the way to school, make sure they got out that day. She used to blot them on the tablecloth to get them posted quickly so we always had these inky patches on the table. Mum put a cigarette in the envelope and these cigarettes used to travel the world: Australia to George, Italy and Africa to Alf. Also we had a tradition of Christmas puddings so every Christmas she used to make masses of puddings and wherever they were, she would try and send them a Christmas pudding, out to the middle of Africa! She used to send these Christmas puddings all for sixpence. Steve said "It's better to send a sixpence, cos I can buy 20 cigarettes with the sixpence." So if she had a sixpence to spare, she put it in. When they came home on leave, it was always the party. Relief that they were home and tears when they went back.

Sometimes, we would hear from them quite regularly, then the letters would stop; then we would get a pile of letters all at once. Most would be from Steve. His wife lived next door to us so if he didn't write to us he wrote to her. We had news of him as far as he could, but he was on a ship so we never really knew where he was.

I remember receiving their letters. It was exciting. But with the telegram boy, everyone hoped that he wasn't going to knock on their door. I know Mum was petrified when she saw the telegram boy coming down the road, in case it was for us. We often had telegrams because the boys would send one to say "We've arrived back in England" or from George "My ship has gone down and I'll be home". Luckily none of them got hurt and they all came home safe, which Mum was always so very grateful for. She couldn't believe how lucky she was, that they all came back. John was the older of the three of us and once George had gone in the forces, I think John was quite envious of the others all going off, because it was exciting. So he was always the one at the door watching the bombers come over and he was always with my dad. If my dad didn't come down the shelter, he would stay with him.

## The shelter

I don't remember the shelter in the back garden very much. My memories are just of playing in it afterwards. Fred worried so much; because he was in England he knew about the raids, whereas the boys that went abroad didn't realise what we were going through at home. Fred made sure we got an indoor Morrison shelter. It was a big iron table, about 6ft, a big square thing. It took up more or less the whole room. We got the chairs around and that was about it. We all used to sleep under it together: Mum, Dad, John, Dennis and me, squashed in like sardines. My dad always made tea for everyone and we had whisky in our tea to help us sleep. It worked as well. You wouldn't wake up until the morning when everything was over!

## The bombs

I remember being scared when we heard the planes come over. When you are young you realise that your parents are frightened so you get scared. When we heard the doodlebugs everyone held their breath until the sound stopped, waiting to see how near they were. Some of my brothers say you can't remember things like that but because it was so dramatic and everything was so loud, these things stick in your mind.

I didn't watch any of the air raids, I would never have been allowed to be anywhere near them. I would have been in a shelter. John would be with my dad at the door watching. Although it was dangerous, as a child you think nothing's ever going to happen to them. He's your dad and if he was around everyone was safe.

*Was there much bombing locally?*

We lived at the back of the gasworks, and they used to say they were aiming for the gasworks. There were bombs dropping around me. I don't think they ever actually hit the gasworks, but all around all the time.

I remember going into the off licence and seeing all the bottles on the floor. Mum had been serving someone and she had just walked into what she called our parlour when the whole lot came down. She kept telling everyone how lucky she was that she wasn't there.

We were always getting the glass broken out of the windows. When a bomb dropped near us all the bottles came off the shelves in the off-licence. My dad had all his friends around that night for a party. They drunk what remained and just threw the bottles in the heap.

*What could they do financially about that?*

Well, we didn't own the off-licence so it wasn't our problem. We didn't think of things like that. The owner, Mr Matthews, was a very nice man. He was terrified of the bombs, frightened out of his life. He would get under the table as soon as a bomber came.

Dad used to keep the off-licence open late in the evening when he came home from work. When the people working in the gasworks had finished their shift, the pub would be closed so they couldn't get a drink. In the off-licence in those days it was draft beer, so he used to stay open. The local policeman used to come in at night, take off his helmet so that nobody could see him. It was open house.

There was an air raid one day when Mum and I were out visiting my Aunt Priss at Downham. We got to the Downham Estate but there was no shelter anywhere, it was just roads and roads. There was a woman air raid warden who was really huge. She threw herself on top of my mum and me. We just disappeared under this huge woman!

Apart from that I can't remember being out in an air raid. When my sister-in-law was expecting her second baby Mum had to go out in one to get the midwife from Sydenham.

The all-clear was a big sigh of relief that stays in your memory. Mum would give a big sigh, thank goodness for that, and everyone would come to life again. It was most weird. You just started carrying on as you were before.

## Bomb sites

We used to play on the bomb sites. It was good fun. For some reason, we were always building huts. We'd make them out of any old pieces of wood or corrugated iron. There was always someone who had a den somewhere or other and we used to rummage around, seeing what we could find; pieces of chalk and shrapnel and all sorts. It was good because nobody cared what you did. There was nothing to damage so it was very free really. I can understand people doing graffiti now, because we did it and nobody took any notice, it really didn't matter. We wrote over everything. The bomb sites were just a place to meet because everyone would be there roaming around.

There were parks locally, where we could go and play but Mum was always too busy to take us and there was always the fear that there would be a air raid.

## Shrapnel and salvage

Us kids used to go and salvage the shrapnel. It was all collected for scrap metal, for re-use. They used to come round and collect any metal things that you had in the house. I remember Mum had a metal bowl that she didn't hand over and Dad told her off. He was really angry because he thought she should have given it up, but Mum wasn't going to part with her bowl.

A bomb dropped and something came through a bedroom wall in our house. Nobody was sure what it was. It was just shrapnel but we had to have someone down to check that it wasn't a bomb.

## School

I didn't go to school until after the war finished. You could go to school if you really wanted to once you were five, but you didn't have to go. They wasn't taking any more children unless you desperately wanted them to go and my mum never wanted to part with any of us so it was easier to keep me at home. John and Dennis used to go to school.

I feel I missed out by starting late, but then Mum was always one to cling to us anyway. I always hated school. I was terrified and I never realised why until later years. It was probably because of the way I grew up, everyone leaving, my brothers coming home and going again, and then my dad died when I was nine. So I think I was worried about coming home from school, because of who wasn't going to be there when I got home. I can understand it now, I couldn't when I was at school.

## Friends and families

Coming from a big family, you always had someone at home. Steve lived next door and his son was born six months after me, so I grew up with him. He was closer to me in age than my own brothers.

It was so friendly down our street. My dad's friend and his sister got bombed out so they moved in with us for a while until they got somewhere to live. They took all the bits and pieces that they could get out of their bombed house and stacked it all in our back room.

I think you knew people much better then because everyone helped each other. We knew everyone. I meet people even now that I knew then. Bell Green was a close community. It wasn't terribly poor but people didn't have an awful lot so everyone was in the same boat, mostly big families. You didn't know you were missing anything, because nobody else had anything. You didn't realise what you didn't have until you grew up.

There are only three of us in my family now but that was not by choice. I would have had a big family. My son is adopted and by the time we adopted him we were too old to have anymore. I still feel it now sometimes, you feel lonely quite often. It's a strange feeling.

When Steve died we all felt the same, this awful feeling of not being together anymore. Then my next brother died as well and we all feel as though something of us is missing. We don't live in each other's pockets, but we're close. We all care a great deal about each other.

My dad didn't like us arguing. Even though there were so many of us you always had to be friends. It worked because we all cared about each other so much. We didn't want to be bad friends. I do tell my brothers what I think about them but I would hate to fall out.

I used to love the two that were in the navy coming home, I loved their uniforms. They had trouble getting out of them as the tops were ever so tight. They had to be pulled out of them, so I always helped do that. I dressed up in their uniforms. Steve had some made for my younger brothers, off his ship. So I had actual uniforms which fitted. Mum was so proud of them that we were brought up to be proud of them. Dennis and me were only saying recently how we were brought up to think our brothers so wonderful. When we realised they were just human and they did horrible things we were really upset!

I remember one Easter when my brother Fred was home and he decided we would have Easter Eggs. He mixed this concoction up with cocoa. He made these solid Easter Eggs using two dessert spoons. They were ghastly, but the excitement was in making them.

We didn't go anywhere during the war. Southend was my first seaside trip, because I had cousins living there, and that wasn't until after the war.

---

**Even though my young years were all through the war I had a really happy childhood because I always had so many people around me.**

---

Bath time was hilarious. We had a tin bath in front of the fire with an inch of water. We couldn't use too much cos you didn't always have a water supply when standpipes were blown up in raids. Often you had to get water from a pipe down the road. We only had a bath once a week, on Friday nights. Dennis and I had to share the same water and he used to stay in it until it got cold.

I never thought about whether we were a well-off family or a poor family. They all say that I'm spoilt because of being the last one and having all the boys. But even if you had the money, the things were not around to buy. I always felt that I had what I wanted anyway. When we lived at Bell Green we had this room that we called our toy room. The only thing I can remember being in there was an old table. I can't remember any toys. I had a doll's pram and a doll and my dad made us things, but we didn't have an awful lot. It didn't seem important. The house was always full of people so you didn't have time to think about what you didn't have. Mum and Dad always felt they did everything they could for you so that's all that mattered. When the boys came home they always bought me something back. I remember having a blue tin handbag, I think Steve brought it back from somewhere or other. Alf brought me back a pendant from Italy. George brought me a dress from Australia and I wore it and wore it. It was blue and flowery when it arrived, but I wore it until there was no colour left. He also brought me bone chopsticks from Japan, which I've always treasured.

Bill was stationed in Ireland and he brought me home two puppies. It was funny because the dogs just sort of disappeared. As a child I was told they were ill and had died. I believed that until two years ago when one of my brothers told me my mum didn't want them, so they found somewhere else for them. Being in Ireland, Bill often managed to send us a turkey at Christmas, even if he couldn't get home.

**Born into the war**

It was strange you know. I was born into the war, it was there in the background, and then it was all over. It was disappointing because I always wanted to join the Land Army. That's the only thing that I ever wanted to do, to wear the uniform and have one of those hats. *Did you have any conception of what the war was about?*

We just grew up hating the Germans. That was the basis of most of our games. Some of us would be the Germans and some the English and everyone hated the Germans. That stayed with you for a long time until you were old enough to realise it wasn't their fault. I know some of my brothers still hate the Japanese but I don't remember thinking about the Japanese at all, just Germans.

The war was quite exciting as I was too young to realise what could happen. Although I knew people had been killed, it didn't register. I was young enough to enjoy the excitement of my brothers coming and going and things like that.

I think I realised how horrible the bombing was though, because people would come in the off-licence and say what had happened. Wherever my mum went, I was with her. So I used to listen to everyone's tales. When Alf was on leave we would sit around listening to his gruesome stories about dead bodies.

**Staying over**

My mum liked to know that we were at home. She wasn't one to let us out of her sight that much. She would let me go out if John or Dennis was there. She liked to be together so that you could look after each other. My brothers' friends were always in our house. One extra never made a difference to Mum because there was a lot of us anyway. She never minded who turned up. Dennis had a friend called Freddy Smith and I always remember him bringing his own breakfast if he stayed the night. His mum wouldn't expect my mum to feed him.

If you went somewhere you took something with you. If I visited aunts with Mum she would take something along. You didn't expect to be given anything. A cup of tea was fine, but you wouldn't expect to be fed.

I never felt as if we went without anything. My dad usually made us games. He was very good at woodwork. They were shared games that the whole family would play, my dad as well. The thing that sticks in your mind is that whatever you had you shared with someone else. My mum never had an awful lot to start with, but she always managed to send something to the boys, sixpence in their letter or something like that.

The only thing I had was a doll's pram but the boys would always pinch it and hide it to tease me. They always walked off with my pram, with me grizzling behind them. At Christmas time, Mum would put new clothes on the same doll and a new shade on my doll's pram and that was my present. We always had a stocking and, if you were lucky, there was fruit inside or a few sweets. Crisps were quite exciting. When we had a delivery of crisps, my mum always kept some. They came in a tin and she would always keep a tin to one side. Lemonade was a treat as well. We used to wrap farthings up in silver paper and go round to the off-licence. We would give Dad the farthing wrapped in silver paper and he would give us some lemonade or something. We thought he was really taken in with this!

## VE Day

I remember a lot of to-ing and fro-ing but I can't really remember anything being said about it. All my memories are of a lot of excitement with someone always coming home. I remember when the boys were gonna come back we had big banner outside. We put 'Steve' on it if Steve was coming home and then Bill would be coming home, so we would put 'Bill' on it. It stretched from the off-licence to the Bell pub across the road. The road was very narrow then, cos Southend Lane was just a little lane. Our off-licence was where the keep left sign is now.

## Rations

We were very short of food. The boys seemed to do better than us. Fred never came home empty-handed. Alf used to work at the grocery store and one of the girls there was keen on him so she always gave Mum extra. Then there was Fishy, Georgie's mate, if the fish came in he would make sure we got fish.

All my brothers used to send things home. I'll always remember George sending us a big case of tinned peaches from Australia. We had a cousin in Canada on my Dad's side, John Moore. My mum saw his mother and she said, "Write to John, he'd send you a parcel of food." So frantically my mum wrote to him. He sent a few parcels over.

Because of having the off-licence, if the whisky came in the butcher was informed and then my mum knew she would get a joint of meat that weekend. John and Dennis used to go in and say to their schoolteacher, "the whisky is in", and he would swap his tea rations for it.

We always had something to eat, perhaps not always the best things but something. My mum and I were way down the line when it came to food. My mum would go without quite often. Everyone would come home and we would sit down to eat and she would always say "Oh I've had mine". You knew she hadn't, it was just to make it go around. If we had chops or anything like that, I would get an end of the chop and it wasn't until I was much older that I realised that there was another piece that went with it.

My mum was a great suet pudding maker. A rasher of bacon would go in a suet pudding to feed us all and we would get the flavour and nothing else. She would slice it up and you'd think "where's the bacon?" Spotted dick and suet puddings, lots of potatoes and lots of pies. She could make a pie with very little meat, you would get that thick crust of pastry on the outside.

I can't remember being really hungry, but you always had to wait until mealtime. You wouldn't dare go to the cupboard and help yourself. There was only a certain amount of margarine or jam to go around so you shared it. My brothers would try talking me out of wanting it. They'd say all sorts of things had walked over my plate. It worked sometimes. I never really got wise to it. I trusted them completely, you see.

When they come out of the forces none of them had an awful lot and as they got married Mum always tried to get bits and pieces for their homes. She always managed to find something. She would get enough rations together to make a cake or have a spread. Most of them used to come home for Sunday tea and there was always a white tablecloth on, if nothing else.

## An Italian in the family

My brother wrote to say that he was marrying an Italian. He didn't know my mum and dad's reaction but he always thought they didn't approve. That was probably because she was Catholic more than anything. But they accepted her. My dad liked her and she liked my dad, although she couldn't speak any English when she first came. My mum had a strange way of being kind. She made it obvious that she didn't want any of her sons to get married. Whoever they married wasn't going to be good enough, but basically she cared a lot for my Italian sister-in-law. When she was pregnant Mum took her to the hospital to translate, so she was really good to her.

A lot of people still hated the Italians, so Mum had to put up with remarks from people about her son marrying an Italian. Quite a few Italians came over after the war and a lot of people avoided becoming friendly with them, so they all sort of grouped together. My family were really nice to her and they all accepted her and nobody treated her any different to anyone else. I think they were all very fond of her really.

## Heroes

I wouldn't let my brothers out of my sight when they came home. Everywhere they went I was behind them. If they sat down, I was on their lap. I just loved them all so much, because of my mum I suppose. Strange now when I think about it because obviously I didn't know them that well, but because everyone else was so pleased to see them, I was pleased to see them as well. John, Dennis and me used to go down to the station if we knew they were coming home by train. We'd sit there and wait until they appeared. Sometimes they didn't and we would trudge back home, all upset because they hadn't come. Bill was only in Ireland but he didn't come home an awful lot. He looked after German prisoners of war. He had a girlfriend out there anyway, so I suppose if he could get home, he didn't always want to. When he did come home we were over the moon. He was everyone's favourite.

My mum worried such a lot about the boys, but I think my dad suffered more in a way. When they came home he was always so relieved and pleased to see them. Every time the news came on the radio everyone had to stop speaking. You would be glued to the set. Then it would be a discussion on "Is so and so anywhere near there?" I always worried that something might be happening where one of the boys were stationed and when they came home we always asked "Where's so and so now?"

I think the worst disagreements were over who was winning the war, the navy or the army. Three of them were in the army and only two of them in the navy so I think the army always won.

## Gas masks

*Did you have a gas mask?*

Yes, "Mickey Mouse" gas masks, in a box. We never had to put them on. I think we played in them more than anything. We had to take them everywhere we went, you didn't go out without one. It was horrible, a square of copper wire. I think it was quite a novelty when we first got them, it all seemed good fun. Terrible really.

Our rugs were always made of khaki and all our blankets were army or navy blankets. I remember having a dress of yellow parachute silk.

## The famous apron

We had a leather settee and armchairs, cos my dad was in the antique business. Everything we had was antique which my mum hated: to her it was second-hand. When my dad died she threw it all out, everything except the settee.

We had a water pump in the garden. *The Mercury* came along and took a photo of my mum standing at the water pump. Just recently they republished the photo. They didn't have her name but somebody in the family saw it. It just had about the water pump and how the lady in the photo was dressed as she would have been in those days, and it tickled me pink because it was the wrap-over apron which my mum just lived in. Whatever she had on, she always had that apron over the top.

# BILLY
## under the Japs

Billy Welch was born in Childers Street, Deptford in 1923. His earliest memory of the area is of "running behind the baker's cart down the Orchard, and getting a ride on the back."

He went to Creek Road School until his family moved from the main Welch residence at Blackhorse Road to Prince Street, down by the river.

A few years later they moved again – this time out of Deptford, to the cottage estate of Downham, six miles south.

The story is a typical one, not only for the Welches but for a whole generation of Deptford families. "A lot of our family moved down there, the Moores, the Whites, the Spooners. They gave us a bath to keep the coal in, we really went upmarket!"

For everyone who undertook it the move meant uprooting from the crowded but neighbourly urban streets for a new life 'in the country'. But, at least for the men and boys, it rarely meant an end to the Deptford connection.

I went to work in the sawmills with my cousin, Jimmy Welch, down Calders at Deptford. I was there for a while then I went to another sawmill, Tytherleigh's down Creekside. I used to hold the wood up for the sawyer to cross-cut it and help out in the yard, lifting the timber about. I used to take bundles of wood up to Nan at Prince Street. I was working there when the war broke out on that Sunday morning. I was about 16.

Our mum went down hopping the day it broke out. They knew it was going to be on but it was a Sunday morning. I didn't go cos I was working. I went down there on my pushbike at weekends, every week after that. I used to go on a tandem with Aunt Doll's husband Bill. Packed up my gear in a backpack, take the grub down to Mum and the kids.

After the sawmills I went to work on the coal lorries, travelling all over London delivering coal, or coke, to the army and the bus garages. Then I went on the building for a while but the governor saw fit to sack me cos I was messing about with Jimmy Todd: just what kids get up to, jazzing about all the time, nothing wicked. Jimmy Todd was a stevedore. There was a lot of stevedores come out on the building. My old man was one. So I knew a lot of stevedores even before I went up the docks.

## Joining up

The Labour Exchange sent me to different jobs but they weren't giving me the money I was getting on the building so I wouldn't have it. They sent me to a job up London. Didn't go much on that cos I had to get up too early and London was a long way away. So I wanted my cards back, didn't want to stay there. The Labour Exchange bloke came round, gave me a talking to: "You've got to have this job." "But I don't want it," I said. "Well, don't work too hard," he says. Well, what's the point of me going up there and not working? I wasn't worried about working hard, I'd worked hard before, I just didn't like going up there. Me and my mate was always late. We missed the Workman [cheap train fares early in the morning] and we had to pay full fare, so that wasn't leaving a lot of money. Anyway I jacked it in. Then I couldn't get a job after that, they wouldn't let me have one unless I went back there. So I said "No, I'm not going, I'll join up before I go back up there" and I joined up.

The day I joined up I got another job, in Downham! I worked for 10 days or so, putting air raid shelters in. It was 1941 and the bombing was well and truly started. We used to have bombs over there, outside the house. Our house backed onto the Downham fields. There was quite a bit of bombing down there. You had to dodge between all the unexploded bombs when you went to get your dinner, which was cooked for us at the Downham Tavern.

I used to sleep upstairs during the blitz. Then I went out one morning and saw all the craters from the bombs dropped the night before. "All right, I'm going down the shelter now" I thought! I don't suppose I stayed there long, at that age you just didn't bother. You used to go out, bombs dropping all round you, you couldn't stay in all the time like hermits.

## Training

I joined the Air Force as a ground-gunner. I enjoyed the training, foot-slogging and all that. The Air Force trained me at Yarmouth, marching up and down the streets. Then the Army trained me at Whitley Bay near Newcastle on a great big golf course where they taught us gunnery. I chose that job; it was bit more romantic than being a window cleaner! They did have window cleaners in the army, general duties in other words. But looking back I think to myself I should have gone into something else because we never learnt anything except gunnery, whereas there were so many trades in the Air Force it was marvellous, you could have come out with a trade for life.

I signed up for the duration of the war when I was 18, but I wasn't educated to know about regiments. I'd wanted to go in the Royal Army Service Corps which was at Dulwich. I only joined the air force because my mate Arty Foskett said "if you join the air force I'll come with you". I agreed because at least I'd have someone to join up with. But we only stayed together for our foot-slogging and the army training. From there I went to London, to a gun post in RAF Fighter Command. He went to Huntingdonshire and I saw no more of him.

I was at London for a couple of weeks. Being the youngest and the newest they sent me to go abroad, which is a sore point. They should have sent the others before me because they were more used to it. They sent me cos I was the odd man out, just come in and interrupted all their systems; first in, last out.

*Who was in control of who got sent?*
Probably the sergeant in the billet was in control. He'd be told, "We want four of your boys" and he would choose. Me and a bloke called Banks came in together and we both got sent overseas. There was people who'd been there a long time before me who stayed. I don't know what happened to them afterwards. At the time we had to take it with a pinch of salt, but we felt a bit niggly about it.

*Was class a big thing in the air force?*
Not really, no. Sergeants thought they was a bit above but they weren't really when you come down to brass tacks. Might have been some people better off than me, a bit classier! But in the forces there's always that thing about 'the lads'. It's all done at low level, it doesn't come from the War Ministry.

**The joys of foreign travel**

They sent me abroad, first to the embarkation point near Liverpool. Then they sent us to Greenock in Scotland and we got on a ship. On December 8th, the day after the Jap war was declared, we sailed. Course, we didn't have a clue where we was going. The trip was all right. It was a big Royal Mail ship, the *Athlone Castle*. It was a lovely ship, it must be marvellous in peace time.

We went to Freetown, Sierra Leone. We chucked a few dud coins over for the 'Glasgow tanner boys', all the natives who come out to the ship. They'd ask for Glasgow tanners and they'd dive into the water for them. Well, we didn't have any Glasgow tanners, so we used to chuck all sorts of foreign coins. They used to say "You messed me up, boss!"

We was in Freetown on Christmas Day. From there we went to Durban and we could get off there. We was there for four days. They gave us half a quid. That half a quid didn't last me and my mate Titch five minutes. We spent it in the first bar we come to and we was broke after that. We was always broke on the ship anyway. Some blokes had hundreds of pounds. I don't know where they got it from, but they had enough to buy tobacco and chocolate.

DICK: *It was unlucky that you was a Welch and brought up in the wrong fashion, a boozer!*

Well, the first day ashore in Durban, me and Titch had spent our half quid. We didn't have any money to get dinner so we went to the WVS or the Church Army to get cake and that. When we got back to the ship, they said "How did you enjoy your day?" The rest of them had had such a great day. People from Durban used to meet the blokes at the gate and take them for a day's outing, ply them with all the goodies and take them home to tea. We'd missed it! We didn't get a sausage!

We shifted off that ship and went onto one called *The Andes*. I got another half quid out of that because it was so disorganised. Someone said to us: "Would you like to do my guard? I'll give you half a quid." We had the half quid, Titch went to see the sergeant to tell him we were there and we shot off after that and spent the money. That was our lot, we didn't have nothing else like that.

**Riot in the ranks**

After that we went on a ship called the *City of Canterbury*. Previously it was an

Italian prisoner of war ship and it was absolutely rotten, full of rubbish. We were supposed to sleep in their hammocks. Filthy it was, running alive with cockroaches. We refused to get on and there was a riot. Shots were fired by the officers. I slept in a shop doorway, wouldn't get on the ship. Matt was right by the bloke who did the shooting, and he heard the officer saying "use your bayonet, man, stop them getting off". The bloke was nearly crying. He ain't going to use his bayonet, is he?

Next morning we went to see what was going on, cos you didn't want to be had up for desertion, no matter what the ship was like. One of the officers gave us a speech. He said "I'm going to tell you where you're going, and you're needed. You're going to Singapore, this is one of the last ships to go in. It's up to you." Most of us dived back on again, actually we nearly turned the ship over, as we all jumped on at once. Some of the blokes stayed behind, they got arrested and sent to a place in South Africa and had quite a nice time actually. The Sergeant was made the scapegoat. They punished him. A lot of the blokes went to India. I never saw anything of my mate Titch after that.

## To Singapore and Java

We weren't long on that ship, straight to Singapore although we had to dodge all the torpedo ships and subs. We landed on Singapore with a bit of a skirmish, bombing us in there. When we got in some of them unloaded the ship. I was on the gun post. Some of the soldiers got off. Mostly all the air force stayed on. We was going to Java, although we didn't know that at the time. Got rid of the poor army. The Japs was within walking distance and they went straight into it.

When we got to Java they bombed us, just strafing over the ship. They sent us to a camp in Batavia (Jakarta), then out to different places in Java. Mind you we didn't know where we were, no one had enlightened us, could have been down Deptford Broadway as far as we were concerned. We heard we were in Java but no maps or nothing, hadn't got a clue what the island looked like, hadn't even heard of it.

## Surrender

We didn't have any aircraft. There was supposed to be a ship bringing planes out but we don't know where they went. Java was the Dutch East Indies and just as I got there the Dutch Government capitulated so that was that, we had to obey. It wasn't us that surrendered which a lot of people think.

As we were going up into the hills the Nips come over with 27 planes, high up in the sky. We was all ground gunners and we had our lorry with the gun on it. We dived off and set our guns. Still the planes were high up. All of a sudden: "Don't fire! Cease firing!" We hadn't even fired yet, they were too far up. Then they said, "Your fighting's over. They've capitulated."

We had to go to a place called Camp Pamegatan for the English officers to surrender. We destroyed as many guns as we could and then from there we was prisoners. We was ordered by our officers to go to such and such a place in Java. Saw three or four Hurricanes shoot across the square just before we got taken but I never saw another one.

## First camp

Eventually we got to a camp where we stayed and prepared the 'drome which had been bombed by the Japs when they were taking it. We was there for six months or more, filling these holes up. Looking back on that camp we weren't treated too bad, though we got whackings and it was the first time we were under the Japs. We got hidings if we didn't salute, even if you didn't see the officer. You'd be walking one way and there'd be an officer somewhere behind you. Because you didn't salute, he'd come over and give you a right belting. He could be a long way off but you still got a tanning.

You had to have your hair shaved off and God knows what. Wing Commander Alexander, one of the Japs wanted to cut his hair off and he went to hit the Jap. They grabbed him and put him in solitary confinement. As we marched round to the 'drome we could see him in this little building. We couldn't speak to him. We didn't hardly see anything of the officers in any case, they was up one end we was up the other. We had to go and work on the 'drome all day in our G-strings and our straw hats. We knew they was eating well up the other end and we wasn't. We only had rice and soup but it was ample, not compared to what we were used to, but adequate.

Most of them who was in charge of us were tea-planters. That's how it seemed to us. One of our officers was a tea-planter in Malaya. He couldn't even tell you how to put your rifle on your shoulder, and he was old.

The Japs didn't talk to us or anything. If we didn't do what we were told we got whackings. We didn't always understand what they wanted. That was the problem. Eventually I learnt a bit of Japanese but that was in Japan.

### The first burial

Then we went to another camp. That was where I buried one of our first blokes that died. I said "I ain't got no clothes to go to a funeral" but everyone lent me things: a hat and a belt and trousers. I looked quite smart actually, though the dead bloke didn't think much of it. We buried him in a nice big cemetery in Batavia. He died of everything: pneumonia, beriberi, starvation; he didn't have the will to fight. We'd marched a long way to this second camp and he was the first one to give up. He was one of us six mates who all kipped together on the floor of the first camp as prisoners.

Gradually people were getting ill. I had Singapore Ear, where the heat does something to your ears. You just sit there, you can't do nothing else, it was so painful. I had a tropical ulcer on my leg, just one little one. I looked after it, but blokes used to have big ulcers with maggots in them.

I was getting thinner but I was still fit. The grub wasn't what we were used to but it was ample, plus what we could nick off the natives. The Javanese used to come past the camp with their baskets of bananas and little loaves and things. We used to go out at dusk when the Nips weren't about. They'd call out "Johnny, Johnny", and show their little cucumbers and bread. Everyone had foreign coins, not Javanese. One of them would pass food through the gate and we'd give him the money. It'd be murder when he found out what he'd got. He'd run up to the guard, but the guard didn't know what he's saying. So he's screaming "They're nicking all my grub" but the guard just gives him a clump.

But really that camp wasn't bad, it was just beginning. We used to go over the 'drome of a night time and cut a bit off of the old wrecked planes and propellers to make air plane models out of it. Some blokes was really good at it. They used to sell them to the officers, hence they still got lots of money. We never saw the proper funds we were supposed to have – station funds, military funds for your comfort and that.

### Officer Bevan

The officers would buy stuff every day, loaves and eggs and what have you. You never saw the officers, only on parade. Except one, I must give Officer Bevan his due. When I had that Singapore Ear I was just sitting on the floor. I looked up and there was him standing there, smart as if he was going out on the town. Someone had polished his buttons up and his boots. "What's the matter with you, young man?" He was only a young man himself. I told him I had Singapore Ear. He said, "You got any cigarettes?" I said "No" and he gave me eight or nine fags. So I had one on the quick and saved the rest to share with the others when they came in. I will admit to him, he gave me some fags, and I still know his name.

## The Danichimaru

They sent us down to catch this boat, this fishing ship called the *Danichimaru*. We didn't know where we were going but we went to Singapore from there. That weren't very nice. You could only come up now and again from down below. The toilets was hanging over the ship. Everyone had dysentery and diarrhoea. That was a bad ship but fortunately we weren't on it for long.

Then we walked, marched, well ambled, to Changi. I spent one night in Changi Jail. They bunged us all in there. You don't get no sense of what's going on. Next morning we went to Changi barracks a bit further on. That's when I first saw a Chinese lady with little feet bound up. Two Chinese ladies came past with their high-heeled clogs. Their feet were so tiny, bound up from when they was born.

I don't know how long we was there, must have been a fortnight or something. We was managing ourselves, the officers were in charge. They had a nice little bungalow, we was in the barracks.

## Confusion

*Were you able to write home at all?*

No, not then. Our mum never heard nothing.

VI: *I was only 14. I was friends with Maggie, Bill's cousin on his mum's side. She used to say "Our Billy's got took prisoner" or "Our Billy's missing"*

DICK: *That's all we knew at home. If the kids were round, you just heard that Bill's captured, someone else is going abroad, and you thought what is it all about. It was confusing really back home.*

Well, it was utter confusion out there. If I wanted to go a certain way I wouldn't know what way to go. We didn't have any maps or anything. All they gave us before we landed in Java was a book called Malay Talk. Well, we didn't want to know about that, did we? We couldn't even read, half of us, let alone speak Malay. You had to ask where the Japs were, how far up the line they were, and all that sort of thing. "When's the next train?" That's useful!

## Sick ships

We went to Saigon, the Mekong delta. We went upriver and they unloaded some of our blokes and materials. Then we come back out again and went to Formosa *[Taiwan]* and some more of our blokes were put ashore there at the copper mines. Then we went to Kobe which you've been hearing about recently with that earthquake.

Meanwhile on the ship they were all dying like flies, dysentery and terrible things. I couldn't go to the toilet and I was quite happy with myself about that. Everyone around me had dysentery.

We nearly got sunk by the big tropical waves out there. Inside a ship you've got a hatchway, then down about 12 foot there's a 'tween deck. All round was all these blokes ill with dysentery and diarrhoea and a far-away look. Then down in the lower hold there was all the really sick blokes. When I come up the first thing I see was Paddy sitting on the tub. He had dysentery and I never saw him off it. He died. Big tall Irishman, hair whiter than snow.

When this wave hit us there were all these sick blokes on the 'tween deck sitting on the tubs. Once you get on there you can't get off anyway because you'd want to get back on again. About 30 of them got killed by that wave. They probably would have died anyway but they fell through the middle hole and landed on the blokes below. If it was a torpedo I'd be dead now, cos I was the last one to wake up. When I woke up there was a commotion in our hold. We was all head to toe right across the ship. They was all running up the steps. I had no chance of getting past them.

There was Yanks and Aussies down there with us. This ginger bloke from Wolverhampton was right over in the bulk head. That was where he used to sleep. But he had dysentery, so he was getting up in the middle of the night. It's pitch dark and black as the ace of spades, and he's got to make his way to the toilet up the stairs. He's only gone a couple of yards when he let go...right across the Yanks! I knew who it was. They're all shouting and I'm killing myself laughing.

*Did you have any way of washing yourselves?*

No, I can't recollect ever washing on that ship. We was on there a couple of months.

## Train across Japan

March 8th I got caught, six months in Java, then to Singapore, another month gone. Landed in Kobe near enough December 7th. It was getting cold then.

We landed there and got Shanghaied onto the train and we was five days on there going right up to the north of Japan, north of the main island. I still hadn't been to the toilet. Might have been psychological – "I ain't having none of that, I'm keeping hold of it!" On this train an Indonesian was sleeping next to me. There was this terrible smell. I didn't tumble it cos we were near the toilets. But it was him, he was wiping himself and bringing back his towel with him! I called him everything when they told me.

They used to stop at all the stations so the Japs could come and look at us in the train, their victories, to show how good they are, all the white men taken prisoner.

## Colder and colder

Then we went to this place called Ohasi, near Khamaisi in the northern part of the main island. It was a new building actually. To us it was nice after the ship. It was very cold there. All of a sudden, the first night there, I want to go to the toilet. I'm upstairs on the first floor, right up in the mountains. I flew out from where I was kipping to the toilet. At the top of the stairs there's a Jap guard, wouldn't let me through. "I want to go the toilet". I might as well have said "I want to go to Kingdom Come", he couldn't understand me and I couldn't understand him. I'm calling him everything. Eventually he let me go down the stairs. When I got in there it was just full of ice. The taps was on and it had all frozen. So I want to go to the toilet and I've gone running in there and I've gone "whhum" and slipped from one end to the other. That was my lot. When I come back I called him a few more things.

We was there for a few weeks, building another camp down the line. Some of the blokes went into the mines. I used to have to go up in the mountains, blowing the face of the cliff away and collecting the stone. That was a cat and mouse game with the Nips cos they wrote up on the barrel how many loads you've got. So you used to half fill a barrel and while he ain't looking whip and empty it and put another mark on it. One day 'the English no good', one day 'the American no good'. We was dumb but they were a darn site dumber.

## Christmas Day

Just before Christmas we landed in this camp. My name's Welch and W is in the last section. They said they wanted so many men to go to work, and some were left out of it. I was left out. Christmas Day come and Captain Zeigler come round with cigarettes. I said "Where's mine, then?"

"Who are you? Did you go to work?"

When I said "No" he said there weren't none for me. I said "Ain't you got no idea of common sense or shares? You never picked me to go to work, now you're not giving me no fags." He was our Captain, a Yankee. He was the highest ranking allied officer. There weren't any English officers. So I had a row with him, saying his principles were no good and what chance have us Englishmen got with him there. I didn't get any off him, but the blokes gave me fags. But that was beside the point. It should have been "Right, you can have nine fags each and those that didn't go to work, take one out of each pack". A bloke couldn't help not going to work.

## Firewood and snow

Well, when I got sent to work, the first couple of days we used to go up in the mountains collecting firewood. In the summer the Japs used to go up and cut trees. We had a little chair fixed onto our backs and a bit of rope. We'd lay all these bundles of wood onto the chair and out onto the rope and then stand up and pull the rope over. You had to take as much as your rope would hold. Going down the mountains, we're slipping all over the show, losing half of our wood after foraging around in the snow getting it. There was one blessing, it was warm when we come down. We enjoyed it really. You were cold going up but when you got back you was really warm.

We used to do things round the little village, doing the roads and pick-axing. The blokes from the mines used to drop all the stonework into this hopper with ice and snow under it. I worked with a Yorkie bloke. We didn't have any proper shoes, it was all toes hanging out. We had to collect all the bits of rock up, put them on this mat with a loop on each end and carry it out through all the slush. "We'll never last this war out here" he said. Up to our eyes in snow and ice. We just had Jap clothes, the trousers up to your shins. We used to cut a blanket up and wrap it round our feet.

## Moving again

We had no idea how the war was going. Although I knew I was in Ohasi, up in the mountains, I didn't know any more than that. The officers might have known a bit more. We had to build this new camp. The ground was harder than concrete where it was frozen. You'd put your pick in and it used to bounce back.

Eventually we built this camp but I didn't have more than a week in there. They brought some sick prisoners to our camp and took us back to the island farther up. There was Americans and

*PoW camp. Billy is second from right, back row*

Australians with us. I'm still in touch with some of them Australians.

## Settling down, getting through

We got to Acardati, a port in Okado. We was there for about two and a half years, loading little boats with baskets of coal. You had to run up planks, across the hold of the boats. They was tall because they had a shallow draught. With nothing in they were like skyscrapers. You had to walk right up the plank. The art was, get up on the plank and drop the load as soon as the boat tips over, then you've not got so far to run. As it fills up it levels off and then it's something like sane. All our baskets used to have to be weighed. They wanted so many tons of coal on this boat.

I got to know some of the Nips a bit in that camp. When we first knew them they was terrible but gradually you got a rapport like you'd get with anyone. Like prison guards here, you hate the sight of them but you get one right one and you'd be on friendly terms with them. We had a vicious governor in charge of us. We used to call him 'Welder's Chops'. He was like an ape, with silver and gold teeth. He used to have ear-muffs and a big sheepskin or yakskin because it was really cold. He did look formidable.

---

**Telling you this is making it all light-hearted, but it wasn't light-hearted. It's all softened now after 50 years.**

---

If I was to talk to you all day and all night you couldn't get what was in our minds, what we were suffering, how cold we were. Most of the time I tried to brush it aside. Others didn't, some just died, give up.

*Did you talk about home a lot?*
Yes, we was always talking about grub. A thousand and one menus and nothing to cook.

*Did you ever think maybe Japan would win the war and you'd be stuck there?*
No, I knew they wouldn't win in my own mind, cos we used to tell the Japs that. They used to be tickled pink, they wouldn't believe it. They would say "London was bombed last night". We'd say "yeah, we know that. But your turn will come next, not very long, Tokyo will be bombed." They'd be laughing, thinking it was impossible. They just couldn't see that it could happen to them. They said if Japan lost they'd kill us and they would all kill themselves as well. But they didn't, did they?

## 'Crime' and punishment

We used to do a lot of thieving. If we got caught, we really got a tousing. I spent 10 days in the guardroom with 27 others. We could only just stretch out sitting down. That was for thieving a load of fish from the ships. We would eat it there, raw salmon out of the icebox. You know the comics, where all you see is the head and the bones? Well that's how we used to leave it. Minutes ago it was fish. They called it masi and saki. We just used to rip the skin off and eat it. If you was down in the lower hold near the engine room, it was always warm. They got snug there and half cooked. But really salty, and nothing to drink.

*Did it occur to any of you to try to escape?*
Yeah, two. They got caught. One in the first camp he got caught. He was a funny sort of bloke. He died in the finish. He escaped and told the Japs he didn't have any friends and that's why he tried to escape. But there was nowhere to escape to, it was all mountains and snow, and nothing to nick. You couldn't go in the sweet shop and nick a half pound of biscuits. You stood out like a sore thumb anyway, even if there was a shop. We had boats nearby but where would we go? We didn't even know how to sail them. And of course you'd have to go past the bit where the guards were. The Japanese navy outside, and all islands out there – you wouldn't know which one to head for.

You couldn't go to the toilet when the roll call was on. In the winter, they did it in the camp when it was dark. No-one's to move until they hear the bell go. I've got to go to the toilet and I can't wait for him to ring the bell. So I shot down the toilet. As I got down there I saw a guard get back into the shadows. I thought, "Oh, he's caught me, the Jockey. He ain't bad though, he don't hit you no more." He had gouged his arm on his bayonet when he hit one of our lads. But now I've started the ball rolling. They've all followed me, they're all going to the toilet. "Watch out, the guard's out there." So I stayed and stayed. I thought if I waited long enough he'd get the hump and walk off, but he didn't. When I come out he screams "guardroom". When I got there there was the Chocolate Soldier and the Yankee Clipper, the two guard commanders. Chocolate Soldier was a proper soldier, the Yankee Clipper loved to whack you, more the Yanks than us, hence his name. "What you doing down here" they said. I told them and I said "I had to go". Oh no, Japanese don't do that, they just do it in their trousers. No, I said, "that's untidy, that stinks, that's dirty, filthy" – all in their own language. So I got a whacking for that. I was determined I wasn't going to give way to them. In the end it got to me saying if Tojo was there or Hirohito was there and I wanted to go to the toilet, I would go. Same as in England, if the King was there you could still go. I got them so wild when I mentioned Tojo and Hirohito, I was just trying to say that was how it was in England, but that was an affront. Two nights I was there and they really went to town on me, punching me, but I wouldn't fall down, otherwise they would put the boot in.

**Billy Bennett and the cigarettes**

Billy Bennett, he was a right one. He was the guard that come to our first camp and transferred the others. One of the blokes was talking to us and he came up and he kicked the life out of him, just cos he was talking to us. Billy Bennett was a film star whose eyes used to roll, that's what this guard was like. When we got to the new camp, he used to tell us "all men got siker jugi". That was Red Cross. When we got there there wasn't much left. But we did get some cocoa. All night you'd see blokes getting up, mixing the sugar and the cocoa and spooning it in.

In this camp we used to have to do night guard in case of fire. They were really afraid of fire. Junior told me he'd been on guard and Billy Bennett came in. "Ah, sit down, I understand you've got no cigarettes."

He could speak good English, which we taught him. He give Junior a fag and said "Want a light?", lit his cigarette. No sooner had he gone out the door, he come back, caught Junior smoking and knocked hell out of him for it. Couple of nights later I'm sitting there on guard. Soon as I hear him coming I shot up. "Ah, sit down. It's cold, isn't it. You got any cigarettes?"

"No, I haven't had a cigarette for a long time."

So he gave me one, then he says "Want a light?"

"No, I'll save it for tomorrow." He was really choked!

When Billy Bennett come through in the middle of the night you had to bow to him and say "I'm the night watchman. I've got nothing to report." We never used to say "Fu Shinbun Fu Ku Matu. Ijo Ari Masen", we used to say "F You Too, Nothing To Report."

**Writing home**

*When did you first manage to get a letter out, or receive a letter?*

Oh, it was about a year before the war ended, I think. And about the same with the old girl, she got a letter to me, or a small card. I think it's somewhere here. I only had a couple. My sisters have got them. I've lost a lot but I've got a little Japanese pipe upstairs what I had when I was prisoner, and my chopsticks. They used to have tobacco that we called frog's hair, it was so fine and as it got older it turned to powder. You used to poke it in this little tiny pipe, get it alight, have a couple of draws, tip it out and fill it up quick and get a light off that and so on and so on. There's a bloke where we go to our reunion, he's got a packet of it. I said "You're getting on now, you'd better let me have it!"

*What did you say in the letters?*
Well, you couldn't say anything. Just said "I'm all right Mum. How's Dad and the kids?" That was your lot. You had to say you were all right, whether you were all right or not.
DICK: *Some of the cards were printed out with things like "I'm sick/I'm well, I've received mail/I haven't received mail, Hoping to see you again..."*

## Staying out of the mines

From Acardati I was transferred again, further north, in the spring of the last year of the war. Some blokes had to go down the coal mines. I thought to myself "I ain't going down there". I had to figure a way not to go. I'd been in dock with beriberi, really bad with it. When we got to this new camp, it was 'all men on parade' to see who's fit for the mines, who's fit for the farm and who's fit for campwork. There was a medical orderly who we called Itchy Cent. He dropped a one cent piece once and he couldn't get over it, he's lost it, he's gotta find it. When you go sick of a morning, whatever you say to him he used to say "Ugh, work". I see Sergeant Smith go to him, he'd been in dock with me with beriberi. We hadn't finished being beriberi. We still had it but not so bad. And Itchy Cent went "ugh, konai", that's the mines. And then he went to Jack Rosebere and I was as bad as him. Ah, he went "camp". So that's 50-50 chance. I thought, "Well I'll have 100% chance. I'm going on the farming parade", so while they was all arguing I just walked over to the farming parade. I was determined I wasn't going to go down the mines, I'd have broke my legs first.

## Farmwork

Ten of us had to pull the plough, cos the horse collapsed. I was in the shafts and I was the horse, cos I was one of the strongest ones there. I had to try and make out I wasn't strong but you had to do it because the others were all weak. We used to have to take the benjo down there to put on the farm, from the toilets. The Japanese have a hole in the ground, no lovely plumbing like us. Someone with a stick and a tin on the end used to have to scoop it out and put it in this barrow. It was like a local dustman that came round to people's houses.

We used to spread it on the fields. You could almost see the plants grow. You would put potatoes in or seeds or whatever. Next morning you'd see ammonia coming up out of the ground, then in a couple of days the shoots would come up. I used to be in the shafts, guiding it round the ruts. Then we had to dig the ground over. With being a lot fitter, I couldn't make out I was ill, even when the Japs were round, you forget yourself. There was an English officer born in Japan and the Japanese consul *[sergeant major]* would say to him "665 is all right to go down the mines", not realising I could hear what they're saying. I was saying "You'll be effing lucky, sir". Treated him with contempt because he never used to come and see us. Nor did any of the other officers, never come down to see how you was.

## Not with a bang but with a whimper

*How did it finish?*
Just like that really. We used to get up at half past four in the morning, have our cup of soup and bowl of rice and out. We were out digging all day long. On this day the consul said "All men camp not come back until it's dark". We thought "Blimey, it's like a nightmare". All of a sudden, "All men camp come back" in the middle of the afternoon. When we got back the blokes in the camp said "See anything out of the ordinary?" There was

always someone in camp, the night miners or the day miners. "Well," they said "the night miners haven't gone out." "So what's up then?" They said there was a fall in the mine, but I said if there was a fall in the mine they'd have them all down there clearing it up. That got us all thinking. In the morning we went down the farm as normal. When we come back they hadn't gone out again. This time they said there's gas in the mine. That ain't gonna stop them going down there. So it went on for about a week or maybe more. Then suddenly the commandant had us all on parade and he told us "Japanese emperor has decided to end the war". It was after August 14th VJ Day. We did know that they'd invaded Germany and the continent but we didn't know much more.

*How long did you have to wait till you could leave?*

Well, I don't know the actual dates, I never used to keep a record. I just shut my eyes and come what may. Some blokes have got dates of different things. I didn't even have a pencil.

He told us the war had ended. Next morning all the Japs had gone. Outside our camp were the Koreans in their forced labour camp. So we weren't getting any grub. But he'd told us that the war had finished so we thought, "Oh well, we'd better go out and forage for it". So we all went over the mountains getting different things. Blokes was bringing back goats and all sorts. We killed the camp pig, hit it on the head with a sledgehammer, that was one of the Yanks. Old Smithy, he's got his knife and the tin, cut its throat and collected the blood to make black pudding. I don't know if he made it. In fact I don't remember eating any pig either. I got plenty when I went out, chickens and eggs and tomatoes, from up in the hills. When I got back to camp I couldn't eat it cos I'd been stuffing myself outside.

### Coming home

When I came back to England, it was a bit dull really. Thinking it was going to be all bright and shiny over here but it wasn't. Everyone was without here anyway, nothing to show, couldn't get any clothes. It was a bit dull, compared with before I went away. Although we were poor we could get plenty of grub. You could get a suit and a pair of shoes if you had the money. Afterwards things was all on coupons. They told me about the flying bombs which I hadn't seen before I went away.

### Talking about it

I talk about things but whatever I say, I can't tell you all the things because in my own mind I can't bring it all out. Some blokes can, they can bring it all out. I had a jock next but one to me who used to have me in tears when we was prisoner, telling us how bad off we was.

We never got no counselling or things like that. Just a medical: "You're all right." "No, I've got a bad..." "No, you're all right." They just give you a cursory medical then on your way.

It wasn't a laughing matter, although we did joke among ourselves at the time. A lot of it was all serious cos you had to put up with it. Some blokes used to thieve off the others, not many though, I only knew two. They got caught and got a whacking.

*Did it make you feel anything in particular about the Japanese?*

Well, I still didn't like them. But I suppose if a Nip come along I wouldn't have hit him or anything like that. I was on the Jap ships at the Surrey Docks after the war.

### Physical reminders

I couldn't sit down on a chair for years. I smashed the bottom of my spine on the back of a motorbike in the second camp in Japan. I was doing a bit of camp work, digging a toilet. We had to go down to town and get some bones for our soup. We was sitting on the back of the motorbike holding these chairs on behind. That road to our camp was all bumpy and this thing didn't have any springs. We went over a bump and I went up in the air, another bump and it smashed on my spine. I couldn't sit down. I had to sit on the floor on a cushion so my spine didn't touch anything.

I've got a fractured disc in my spine. That was a whack from a Jap with a shovel while I was on the coal. That was cos I was talking. This was a student and his mate. They was watching us. We were having a joke and a talk. He smashed me on the back. I went down and I called him everything and he could understand English.

I had that all the time working up the docks but I had to pull my weight to keep the job. I could work normally on timber, but when it was a big case it was hard.

## Settling down a free man

I got back-pay for 3½ years, about £180. That was Japanese campaign money.

*What would that buy you then?*

A lot of beer! I could have put a deposit on a house, but I wasn't educated to that. We never gave it a thought. By the time I met Vi I'd spent nearly all of it. We just had enough left to buy an engagement ring, that was £14. I came back in December. We first went out in January 1946. We were courting for two years, then we got married Boxing Day 1947. We got two rooms for 12 shillings a week. I'd spent all my money and we had a bedroom suite and a dining room suite on the knock, but we cleared it up within a year. The next year we saved up enough for our first motorbike.

Vɪ: *That was what we done then. There was no-one to say "Try for something better". The system was, you got married, you got a couple of rooms, then you put your name down on the council list. That was how it was.*

# ARTHUR and KITTY

## flat coins and cold baths

Arthur was born in 1931, Kitty in 1933. They spent their early years in Granny Welch's house at 48 Blackhorse Rd. The family moved within Deptford to New King Street where they slept eight to a bed.

The children were evacuated to Devon on the day war was declared and had a mixed experience of country life. Although they hated the woman they were staying with, her husband 'Uncle' was their guardian and saviour.

They returned to Deptford in 1941 and, tired from the journey, were only just persuaded to shelter during the raid that greeted them. "It's a good job we did because our house was bombed that night...completely smashed."

Their parents separated during the war and both children remember their hostility towards their father for leaving Mum with seven children. Of all the Welches Kitty and Arthur's family probably suffered the most financial hardship. Whereas the other children remember stews and heavy cakes, Kitty remembers "Oxo in a basin for our dinner".

**Kitty:** When war was first declared, we had to go to Childeric School with labels on and our gas masks and a little bag to take a few clothes. They picked us up from there in a coach or charabanc as we called it then. The school was done out like a rest centre because they had started to get it ready for bombed-out people. We went up to Paddington and went straight to Devon. We went on the 3rd September 1939. The war hadn't hardly been declared.

I don't know how our mum found out that we had to go. She must have had a letter or something. They put me, Arthur and our sister Florrie on a coach and I can remember saying goodbye to my mum. I was crying me eyes out and my sister saying, "She'll be alright Mum, she'll be alright. Come on Arthur".

I was crying half the way down on the train. I must have dozed off in the coach and next thing I knew I was on Paddington Station. I think it was Paddington, a great big one with a glass roof. Then the next thing, we was standing outside in Newton Abbot with a Wagon Wheel biscuit.

The people could choose the children they wanted. When we got off they put us in a little hut which was part of a school and we had to stand in line. We were right at the end. This couple of ladies were looking at us and I said, "Oh, I hope that lady don't pick us, she's just like a witch". She had a long face and grey hair, just like a witch. And what happened? She picked us. She said "I'll have the two girls, but I don't want the boy" so we said "No, we want our brother". We were crying, breaking our heart and my sister's saying "We've got to keep him with us, he's our only brother, he's got to stay with us". When we got into this house, this lady that picked us, Mrs Norsworthy, was there on her own. I said, "Oh no, she's like a witch. Look, quick, look, and she won't have our brother, she won't have Arthur." She took us into the front part of the house, we were never allowed to use that front door. We always had to go around the back. It was dark and dim. She said "Do you feel hungry?" We said yes but I thought "Don't eat nothing. She's gonna kill us". When she came out, she gave us tiny little pork pies, one each. I whispered to Florrie "Don't eat them" but she says "We'll have to, we'll starve". I said "We might not wake up in the morning". Oh God, when I think of that now! Then Uncle *[Mr Norsworthy]* come off the train.

"What's wrong with you, dears?"

"We want our brother."

I was only six, Florrie was nine and Arthur was eight. Uncle said "Don't cry. We'll go along and see if we can fetch your brother for tonight". We went and got him and we all got into bed, cuddling each other, all crying, "We want to go home". Now my mum had said "If you like it there put lots of little kisses and if you don't like it put lots of big kisses".

**Arthur:** Which we did and the old man come down a bit later and took us home.

**Kitty:** We loved the place but the people we were staying with were cruel to me and my sister. The postman that Arthur stayed with was lovely, Mr and Mrs White. They were old people, in their eighties. Mrs White took us out blackberry picking. One day we were out and these three German planes come over and started machine gunning us. Mrs White grabbed hold of us and threw us all into the blackberry bush. I was smothered in blackberry balls.

**Arthur:** We loved it in Devon. It's a beautiful place but when it was cold, it was cold.

**Kitty:** We used to go water-cressing in the streams and we were always in the fields. That was our playground, because it was at the back of our door. You could walk out and you were there. There was always apples peeking out over the top of people's walls and as we came home from school we could just take apples. Nobody moaned or anything like that.

We were there about 18 months. On a Saturday we used to go to the pictures, then when we come out we went to Newton Abbot Park. It was a beautiful park. One day we were all excited and I was running down the steps and I couldn't stop. I just went straight into the lake where the swans were. I actually drowned, I know I did. I'm going under and it's getting darker and darker and I'm looking up and I thought "Oh, I can't live here". I was only seven then and I thought "I've got to get up somehow. What do I do?" I couldn't swim so I just done a doggy-paddle to come up and it was getting lighter and lighter and there was thick slime all down me. Of course, as I come up somebody was waiting for me and picked me up.

Mrs Norsworthy whacked me for that. There was a girl in the park who was going home the next day and we said to her, "Please tell our mum that I drowned".

**Arthur:** That was the same as me. Our school was in between two parks. There was a big swimming pool, and two fish ponds, one deep and one shallow. There was a little kid and his ball went into one of them. Now I thought it was the shallow one and I said to this man "I'll get his ball". So I took my shoes and socks off, went to paddle and went 'Whoosh', straight down because I couldn't swim then. I bobbed up again and he grabbed me. I ran home, and as soon as I got in she said "What happened there?" I said "Well, I went to get a little boy's ball and the man pulled me out". I got the biggest hiding I ever had.

**Kitty:** My mum used to send us parcels. There was always Mars bars in them. Four pieces, one each for me and my sister and one each for the two boys that lived there. But we never saw any of them. She used to give them to her two sons.

If we did anything naughty, just like children do, it would be, "Look at your shoes", and she'd whack us. I used to say "Leave my sister alone. I'm going to tell my mum. I'm going to write and tell her you've been hitting us." She whacked my Florrie. She used to hit her so hard and lock her in the coal cupboard all day and Uncle come home and we were in bed one day. We were all crying up there. He said "Where's Florrie?" I said "She's in the coal cupboard", and he went mad. He was such a quiet man but he went berserk. We could hear him shouting and hollering at her.

Every day we had lettuce sandwiches for our tea, every single day. But I tell you what, that lettuce sandwich was beautiful. I suppose we were bloody hungry.

The day we came home Father give Mrs Norsworthy £10 and we thought "What did he give her that for?" He gave her £10 for looking after us but we didn't get looked after. Oh well, Uncle did look after us. He was nice.

**Arthur:** He was a nice bloke, I used to go on Sundays down the railways with him, on the engine. He was a train driver.

**Kitty:** One day she'd locked Florrie in the coal cupboard and she was crying her eyes out. I was in bed and when Uncle came home I said "We've had a parcel and Auntie won't let us see it". Uncle said "There's your parcel and you do whatever you like with it." Well, we opened this parcel and there was a stack of sweets. Even though it was about half past five and we were in bed, he said we could go out and play. In this parcel there was something for everyone. I don't know what Arthur and Florrie got but I got these white tap shoes. I'd always wanted white shoes. I tried to get them on but I couldn't get them on quick enough and they was a little bit tight. I forced my foot in them and I went out, up the garden outside into the alleyway before you got to the field. All our friends were out there. We're all singing 'Somewhere over the rainbow', and all dancing. We were always acting. They're saying "Oh, aren't your shoes lovely", but they were crippling me.

**Arthur:** The coal man used to come round every Sunday, across the field at the back of our gardens. There were little cottages and the other side of the road was the side of the station. He used to drop this hundredweight, big bloke he was, to the house on the corner. I would help him with it.

One day I was going across and when I looked up, there's about a hundred foot of railway line complete with sleepers coming right over at me. It dropped about a hundred yards before our horse and cart.

**Kitty:** The railway was there, a little tiny road no wider than this house. You cross over and then there's our houses along the railway, all belonged to the railway. We used to go out our back door and right at the back was fields, we always used to play near the back door, in the field. If we'd have been playing there that day, we wouldn't be here to tell the tale now because the railway line was bombed that day. The railway line actually flew through the air. It come over a thirty foot wall.

We had to go to school every morning. The English children came with us, I can remember some of the children that lived there. The two boys that lived with us in the house, Cyril and Roy. Roy was nice but Cyril was a proper Billy Bunter. Roy was very thin, Cyril was as big as a house. About 18 he was. He was so cruel to us. He used to pick holes in us, and he was always pulling faces at us.

## Coming home

**Kitty:** The day we came home it was quite dark. We were indoors in Riley Buildings and I can remember Mrs Dalton saying to mummy "Come on Flo, the warning's gone", someone said "Oh they're tired. We won't go down". Good job we did because our house was bombed that night. Anyway we got down there. In those flats they had one of the big communal ones. We saw all our mates. Oh, it was lovely to see them. We must have gone to sleep, and next we heard that we had no house left.

The house was completely smashed. Everything was down on the floor. The whole of the corner of the four or five flats was down and there was nothing left. There was dust everywhere when we came out in the morning. I can remember coming out of the shelter and everything seemed white. There were firemen and policemen and all different people and different things. I can remember looking round, and someone had hold of me. We went to our granny's after that, to my mum's mum who lived in Rotherhithe.

**Arthur:** There wasn't room for all of us. We used to top and bottom, about six of us in one bed.

**Kitty:** We stayed at granny's for about three weeks. Then we got a three bedroom house, down in New King Street. When we moved back to New King Street after the evacuation, there were eight of us in the bed: us girls at the top and Arthur and the two babies at the bottom. Mummy used to get in as well when it was cold. There was a big hole in the wall in the next room, a massive gap from the bomb damage. Somebody gave Mum a piano and she put it up against the gap.

## Air Raids

**Arthur:** One time we was half way down Blackhorse Road at the end near Molins and there was this bang, maybe 100 or 200 yards away. The blast shook the ground and one of my mates called out, "Where's the bank?". So we ran to the bank and there was all these coins outside. I'm picking up half pences. The most I picked up was four pence but in a few minutes the coppers arrived. A copper come along and he give me such a wallop. Tipped them all out. While he's tipping them out he's backing me up against a wall. I saw an old girl there she picked a wadge of notes up. I said "Go on, girl!" She put it in her bag and walked around to the flats where Gran used to live. I actually saw the coppers picking up wadges of notes and putting them in their pockets.

I finished up with a few bent half crowns. I give me mother a couple. I bought sweets with the rest, all farthing gollywogs. But I didn't half get some whackings off them coppers that day. We all did.

**Fun in Deptford**

**Arthur:** We used to go swimming at Deptford Green, down the Watergate where the Light *[Deptford Power Station]* was until recently. In the summer you could stand with the hot bricks to keep you warm. The electric grid was on one side and the power station was on the other. There was all barbed wire up there. I've seen an arm hanging up from there, from a bloke who was working in the grid.

**Kitty:** There were barges there that we used to play on. We didn't think they was dangerous but they were. Then we had all the Yanks down here. They were nice. They used to give all the children gum, sweets and chocolates. They were really kind to the kids. Then after the Yanks went somewhere else, we had all the Italian prisoners.

**Arthur:** I used to get a carton of fags. I would get half of Porter and half of Burton in a jug and mix it, half Porter and half Burton. It was about a shilling for a pint. We would split open one of those bags of peanuts in shells. Oh, they were gorgeous, raw peanuts straight from the field, bagged up abroad. They was all milky cos they wasn't baked. Our cupboards were full up with peanuts.

**Hop-picking**

**Kitty:** When we came back to London, they said "We're going down hopping". We were all thrilled to bits, "We're going down hopping in the open air". We went down to Barn Hill with Granny Welch and all the crowd. Oh, hop picking was lovely. Everybody knew us.

**Arthur:** We had six months down there during the war. You could do fruit picking, potato picking. I loved that. You stepped outside the square and you're in the orchard, nicking all the apples and pears.

*There was no school presumably for that six months?*

**Kitty:** We used to have the Brown Brothers come down and the Salvation Army. The Brown Brothers were just like monks, all in brown with hoods and sashes. They were lovely. They used to help people, first aid and that.

**Arthur:** They took us to school of a morning. If we never come back with a text with Jesus on, we'd have got a hiding. You had to show them that. I used to go there and nick one and run away so I could say "I've been, look!"

**Kitty:** When we were down hopping they dug trenches so that people could jump in the trench if there was a raid. Every time we jumped in the trench there was big frogs and toads and the boys used to frighten all the girls. We were always screaming. We used to have great fun down there.

We were there for quite a long time and then I came home and went to

Leicester with my mum and the rest of the children, he stayed down hopping. We went to Leicester for two years. Our little brother was born down there.

## Splitting up

**Kitty:** Then my mum, Florrie, me, Sheila, Olive and Maureen went to Leicester. Mummy was going to have Leslie. While we was there we had a letter saying that my father was talking about the trouble women are.

**Arthur:** The old man would hang his coat up and I always went down his pockets, looking for a fag. I was only young and I used to smoke. One time I pulled out a photograph of this tart and him. My mum looked at it and said, "Give us that here". Dad just walked out and then he was living with this other woman at South Norwood. Mother and Aunt Edie went to find him. Aunt Edie nearly broke the door down. She was a tough old girl.

**Kitty:** He came out and pushed our mum and said "Go away". When he pushed her he done something really bad to her knees. I don't know how she got home. Her knees was all swollen up.

Mum had been crying. Aunt Edie came in raving. Apparently they'd caught him living with this woman. Then Mum had to go in hospital. They had told her that all the seven children would have to go into Sidcup homes. My mother said "No way! Please get out my house. Thank you very much, but my children have not got to go into any home. I've had them, I'll look after them. They're my babies and no one in this world is going to take those children." So when she went into hospital Gran had two of us, me and Arthur went to Aunt Lou, Maureen and Sheila went to Aunt Nell. But they didn't like it there and I didn't want to stay with Aunt Lou, so we swapped over. I stayed with Aunt Nell until I got married.

We used to see Dad quite a lot, but we would never talk to him because he'd done a really nasty trick. He used to be in the High Street or up the top of the road, or he might have been coming from his mum's. We never talked to him.

He tried to talk to me once but I was terrified. I was pushing a pram as I had just had a baby. The next time I saw him he was with this woman. I don't know if it was the same woman, but I heard him say "five babies..." I'd had five babies at the time. I was just coming into Douglas Street where they had all the stalls in those days. I saw him, and I thought "oh God!". I was terrified. I was walking along with the babies all in the pram cos it was starting to rain. I used to bung 'em all in there. I heard him say "There's my Kitty". I still didn't take no notice. He said "She's just like her mum, all the babies on the pram". That's the words he used. I'll always remember that. Another time I was going up New Cross Road with Bill when we was courting and my dad was coming along with another man. He said "Hello, Kitty" and I just went "Hello" and walked off.

He worked in the docks as a stevedore. His nickname was Treacle. All the stevedores and the dockers and the lightermen knew him well. He was a nice little man, a dancer. He was handsome, a really handsome-looking fella. He used to teach us to dance when we was little. I can remember him tap-dancing with us. He used to give us our dinner sitting on his lap.

All the dockers knew that he had left my mum with seven babies and they all turned against him. All coming from Deptford, the stevedores and the dockers knew my mum and knew all the families down there.

**Arthur:** All the uncles left their wives.
**Kitty:** Aunt Priss had a hard time. So did Aunt Rose and Aunt Maud.

*What was the attitude towards people getting separated at that time?*
**Kitty:** Oh, it was terrible. When they did find him she used to take him to court to get money to keep us. They used to have a thing called the R.O. *[Relief Office].* They would allow my mum money and

when the police caught him he would have to give the money back to the court. But they could never find him. He allowed my mother half a crown for each for us to try and get a Sunday dinner.

**Arthur:** Mum used to have two jobs. She got a pound a week scrubbing the Osborne in New King Street. Then she would go next door to Sam's Cafe and wash up. There were hundreds sitting down in old Sam's Cafe. It was a big place.

**Kitty:** There was times our mum didn't have nothing. We used to have Oxo in a basin for our dinner. She just did not have the money. Ronnie Davis in the shop was kind. He used to give Mum bread for nothing. People were ever so kind to Mum.

**Arthur:** That place is still there up the High Street, where me and mother went to line up for loaves. It didn't cost you nothing. The loaf was thick. We had second-hand clothes but I used to have a new pair of boots, mind you. She'd never give out second-hand shoes.

**Kitty:** I remember coming home from school and my mum was there with a pile of washing. She'd be scrubbing it on the scrubbing board and there was about six lines of washing all hanging up. Scrubbing, scrubbing, and the sweat was pouring off of her.

On a Saturday she'd take us up Douglas Street. There was all clothes she'd pick out for us. Then there was Uncle Bob. He was the policeman in Amersham Vale. He used to have the stall at the top of Edward Street. It was his stall and he used to say to our Florrie, "Here, take that home to your mum."

## Thieving and punishment

**Arthur:** In Douglas Street there was a stall with beetroots. So I nicked a beetroot. I had done it loads of times but then I see a great big hand. It's the owner. He give me a wallop around the ears and said "Right. I want you up here Saturday morning to work for me". He didn't give me any money though. He told me mother and she gave me a good hiding for nicking. I had red all over me from the beetroot. Next morning I'm looking, he ain't looking, I get the potatoes. He grabbed me again and gave me another wallop. He said "Don't nick. If you want one, ask for one." "Alright Bob." He said, "It's Uncle Bob to you." He was a part-time copper and he was getting a bit too old, about 30. This was in the war. He was a special. He went full-time and after about two years he become a sergeant. Anyway, he made me work on the stall.

I couldn't lift the tables, I used to do three of them and I'd be knackered. I was only a kid. He said "All right, stack all them oranges up". You had to take the newspaper and wrap it on the oranges, undo your wrappings and then make it round and put your orange on top of it, like a cup. They look nice then. He showed me how to do it. The same with bananas. You got to have the little tag on it showing, and they would all be lined up, beautiful. It took me about three hours to do that. I think I packed up about four o'clock on a Saturday. I said "Where's me money?", but he just gave me an apple. He would never give me money. "That's for nicking all my beetroots. Do it again and you'll stop round here all the week when you come home from school, for an hour every day". So I never nicked no more. But I said "Uncle Bob, can I have an orange?" "All right, take one" and I was a devil: I took it right from the middle so they all come down. I got a whacking off him again.

## Rations

**Kitty:** We had ration cards. You had one egg a week and about two ounces of butter. My mum never used to keep the butter. We had margarine. We always had jam if we could get it. We used to have dripping from the meat. We loved dripping. We used to have lard on our bread too, with salt and pepper on it. We never had butter and that's why we don't eat butter now.

**Arthur:** Because there was a lot of us we got rations of a quarter of butter each and two pound of sugar. She used to have two pound to spare and she would sell it for twice as much to the hairdresser. There was a lot of black market. You would sell your clothing coupons.

When I went to the army, it was still on then, rationing and coupons. I used to come home for the weekend on a 48 hour pass. I would go in the company office to get me pass. I was a crook right. He turned his back and I picked up a packet of clothing coupons. You could flog them for half a quid a piece. I had a wadge about a quarter of an inch thick and there was about 50 on each page.

## Army Life

**Arthur:** I was at Wimborne in Dorset. When you first start you have the 17 weeks training to learn your sten and your rifle, before you got your 50 bob, four and a half quid. If I went home that were me fare. When I was coming back Sunday night, Aunt Nell used to give me half a quid. I had a case for me dirty washing. The side used to come out to make it wider and Aunt Nell would fill it full of grub, cakes and sandwiches and whole bread puddings. I said "I can open a cookhouse tonight!"

If I want 12 eggs, I'll eat 12 eggs. Sausages were only allowed one per person, yet I could eat 25 of them. I always used to bring a parcel home every week. We used to say, "Postman, have you got a parcel for me? You go past the police station first, and then I'll take it off you." It would be full of tinned sausages and a big tin of corned beef and something like that. I got 15lbs of tea in one day once.

When I was at Dorset, I used to get up at half past five to start the cooking or me mate Terry did it. He was a chef, I was only a cook. We had the army firemen down there and we used to feed six of them at a time. Then there was the troops. Sometimes it used to be hundreds. We had to count them and then put down what we catered for.

One time the captain says "You going home today Welch?".

"Tomorrow, sir, if I can."

"I don't see why not...Anyway, give us a tin of corned beef to take home."

So I give him a tin of corned beef and I think to myself "what a lovely bit of meat there. I'm going to take that home." My family had never seen a big joint like that for years. Still had the blood coming out of it. So we wrapped it up in greaseproof paper and put it in me case. The coach has pulled out. My mate was in first and I'm behind him. He walked right down the end cos there was no seats here. I'm following him with me case between my legs, rolling it along because it was heavy, full of grub. Suddenly he turns round and says "come up here, quick". When I looked down there was all blood coming out of me case!

"What you got in there?"

"What do you think I got in there?"

"Don't be lippy, you saucy b*****!"

He had a go at me and I had a go at him back. We got there in half an hour and he's going on about it "he's thieving again". I said "Shut your mouth" and sat down besides Captain Yates. He had me when we got back on Sunday night. I said "You got a tin of corned beef and what else did you nick out of there? Like the sausages and bacon gone. My mate Terry caught you."

About a hundred yards down the lane, there was a big old mansion. It was hundreds of years old. It had these candle sticks on the walls. If I'd known how much they were worth, I would have had them off.

## Work

**Arthur:** I left school in 1945, at the very end of the war. You would get a job and pack it up and get another job an hour later. My first job was in Towler's. We used to make tanks, tanks for engines, tanks for water, tanks for beer.

At the side gate there used to be coal. Everyday I would fill up a coal bag, open the gates, run down home, put the coal bag underneath somewhere and hide it until the next morning. Our garden was full of coal.

I used to cut all the railings up and sell it to the breakers for making bullets and guns. We would put it on a two-wheel barrow. A three hundredweight would give you two bob and two bob was a lot of money.

## VE Day

**Arthur:** In 1945 I was 14 and I'd just started work down Towlers. I wasn't there long cos then I went on the building. At the end of the war everyone had street parties all day. All the mothers used to make lemonade and sandwiches. Everything was still on ration but they made it. Even the coppers used to come out the police station to pick up some sandwiches. We had bonfires. We didn't go up town, we all stopped at home.

**Kitty:** During the day we had a lovely party. Our local fish and chip shop man at the bottom of our road laid on fish and chips for all the children. The women ran round fetching their own plates out. We had this lovely fish tea and someone down the docks had fetched up a crate of fruit for us. In the evening a little stage was made in front of someone's house and everybody had to get up and do a turn. We had tried to get some parachute material to dress up with. We couldn't get it anywhere but we got some silver paper. So we had these big silver bows and our dresses were all made with silver paper.

Doreen and Joycie Buckingham and me walked all round Deptford and New Cross in our silver dresses. We came up to the top of Clifton Rise near the Kinema. The road was packed with people and there was Mr Blanchard, the Mayor of Deptford. We followed him around everywhere, and he said "you three girls are lovely". There was loads of press there taking pictures of us, but we've never seen any photos. They must be somewhere in the archive.

Anyway the mayor invited us up to his Chambers with his wife and children. He gave us a little drop of wine. In school that week we'd been given a small box of sugared almonds and one red apple from Canada but when we got into the mayor's rooms he gave us about six boxes of these sweets and about eight apples each. He asked about our families. My two mates were sisters and they told him where their Dad worked. Ted Buckingham worked for Smiths Crisps and he was doing a bit of sooting at the time. Then he asked me so I said "we haven't got a father. Well we have, but he left my mum" and I went right through the story. He wanted to know about all my sisters and brothers and I told him that my mum had seven babies to look after.

The next day this big limousine turned up outside my mum's house. I was living with my aunt, but of course I had to say I was still living with my mum in case she got into trouble. I came round to Mum's just as the car had gone. I saw this big car but I didn't take any notice. It turned out Mr Blanchard had sent the chauffeur down with a brand new pair of Wellington boots for me. It was sad because they didn't fit me so I had to give them to my Sheila. But he also sent a big box of sweets and apples for the family. And I thought, "oh, ain't that nice".

*Did the atmosphere change after the war?*

Oh yes, it started when people started getting money. They was saving up and they wanted this and that and they wanted to be like the Jones. I'm gonna have a new carpet and then you'd hear someone else say "I'm going have one of those carpets" or "I'm gonna get those curtains" "oh, I like those curtains I'm gonna get them". If somebody had something someone else wanted to keep up. As soon as they started getting more money in their pockets people definitely changed. For years after the war they was still friendly because you knew everybody, but then they started altering.

# ROSIE

## home and the hopfields

Rosie was born on 3rd September 1930, so the day war broke out was her ninth birthday.

Her family was blasted out of Blackhorse Road and, although Rosie didn't feel much about the house, she was upset when she found a friend wearing a coat that had been left in there.

There was no-one who could take in mother and six children so they were all evacuated together to Devon.

They returned when they were offered a council house on the Bellingham cottage estate.

Their father volunteered a few days before they got back and was away for five years. Things settled into a surprisingly comfortable existence until his return, which was not quite as welcome as they would have wished.

Rosie has strong memories of hop-picking in Kent. She was there at the outbreak of war and when she was working, just before the end of the war aged 15, she continued to go to the hop-fields at the weekends.

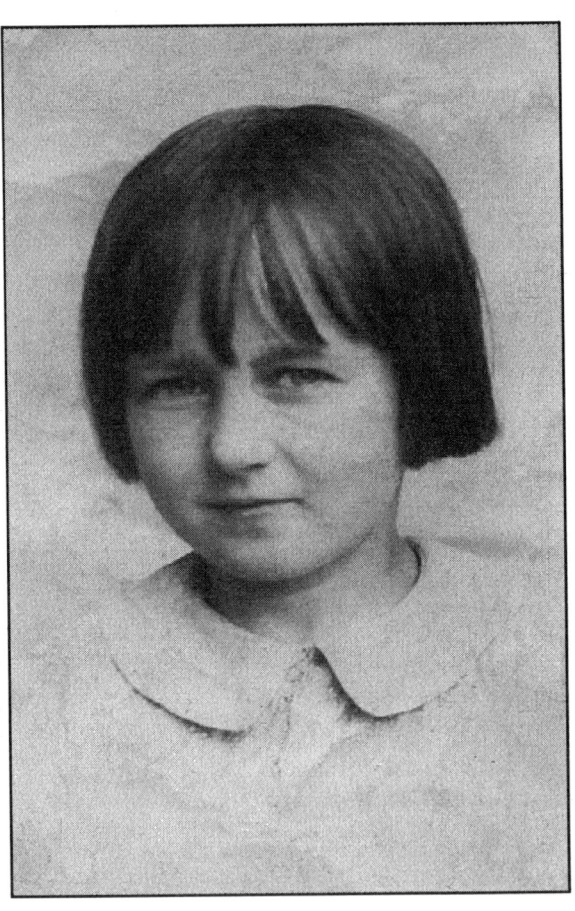

I was hop-picking on the day we first heard of the war. I think there must have been a siren. Everybody ran out to the hill and looked around. The planes went over, towards home. We knew they were going over to London. We were just watching them go. Well, we had Mum over there and all those at home. It used to upset us a bit.

The only time we saw them flying low was when we were in Bellingham and they shot Sandhurst School in Catford. He came as low as our dining room window. You could see the full head of the man looking down at you.

## Hop-picking

We used to go down quite early in the morning, on this big old lorry that the hop-pickers used to hire. It was open-backed with a canvas top, so if it rained you were under cover. We would sit on the floor, Gran and us. We'd take odd bits of wall-paper to make the huts look just that little bit better. We'd pin it to the old wooden walls. All our bits and pieces, saucepans and whatever, we'd pile onto the lorry then go up the road and collect friends and mums and dads. On the way towards Kent we'd pick up my aunties and their children. When the lorry was full up we went to East Farleigh.

Before the war we lived at my gran's in Blackhorse Road in Deptford, Gran down and us upstairs in two rooms, with six children. Then we were blasted out. We moved to Bellingham but my brother and I still went hop-picking with my grandmother. My mother never used to go at the time because my father disagreed with hop-picking.

When the war got bad Mum kept writing to my father saying, "Can I go hop-picking? We've got six children and the bombs are bad." He agreed that time and she went hop-picking. There was my grandmother and about four or five of my aunties all in little square huts.

*How many could you fit in a hut?*

Oh! Quite a lot at a weekend! Cos all the husbands used to come down then. Gran and my Aunt Cag and Aunt Doll, Aunt Cag's husband, couple of Aunt Doll's children, couple of Aunt Cath's, couple of us...16 or 18 in a hut. There was one long wooden bench which was the bed. We used to take the empty mattress-cases and when we got there it was hard work stuffing them with straw.

There was too many of us, you see. The unlucky ones used to make up big bales of faggots, branches, you know, tight round the middle. The old farmer would bring them down during the day and put them in this big square for our fires, to cook on. But if there was a lot of people in the hut then they would be laid on the floor until they reached the bed height and then another bag was stuffed with straw on top of that. And that's where most of the children kipped down.

*And that wasn't quite so comfy?*

That wasn't, no. Especially if the mattress moved and you were lying on those branches! It used to be running alive with bugs and earwigs. There was holes all round the roof and they used to crawl down and drop on you in the night. You'd go "Oh, what was that!?" Oh, never, ever, take up hop-picking!

I loved it! We had to work for my grandmother, she being parted from her husband. My brother and I would have to sit with my grandmother and another cousin Sophie, who my grandmother brought up as a baby. It's hard work sitting there all day long pulling the bines and if it's raining you're wet all over and spiders all over. If we slacked then my auntie would be onto us: "Get on with it. Your Gran's gotta keep you, get on."

One day I wasn't well. The farmer came round and weighed all our baskets. The sacks full of hops that were ready they threw down. My grandmother said "Go and lie down on them, if you're not well". So I had permission from Gran and I fell asleep. Course my aunties were "Nah nah nya what's she laying there for? Why ain't she working?" One of the sons came over and threw some water over me. Anyway when we got back to the hut that evening they had to call the nurse that used to come round on a bike. I'd got this very bad tonsillitis and I was in those huts for a whole fortnight. It wasn't very pleasant when you're on your own, lying in those huts, and they'd all gone hop-picking. A friend stayed some days when I was ill, but then her mother needed her to pick the hops.

You've got your hops growing up the bine. You've got four on each section and two go each way so that you've got rows. You start at the top and go all the way down that row. You've got your great big bin and you pick two this side and two the other. They're right high, taller than the room. They're on a string, growing up it like a runner bean. Granny would pull at the frames of wires that the strings were tied to, pull, pull, until it broke. That length came down and it's full of hops, so you threw it over the bin. By that time you're drowning wet because of the dew that's all over you...ugh, long-legged spiders!

Then you sat on the edge of the bin and you broke a branch off and held the end then slid the hops off half a dozen at a time. Leaves came with them but you had to pick those leaves out, as many as you could. Great big ones had to come out, but the tiny ones you couldn't help. The farmer came round and put his big basket in, and said "one" into the sack, and "two" into the sack. Well, if he pushed too hard, he'd get twice as many. As soon as he did that, Gran would call out "Eh, come on, you're pushing them in a bit aren't you?"

You got sixpence a basket. But if you had a lot of leaves he would say "Too many leaves" and he'd put more in. So the cleaner they were the less he had to press them in.

*Did you come back when the war started?*
Oh no, we stayed there. Hop-picking didn't change very much because of the war. The men never went during the week anyway. They only went down by train on a Saturday. I remember going to meet them from the station.

When I left school and went to work, just before the end of the war, I used to go just at the weekends. I'd go to Bromley and catch a train to Kent.

When we were down hopping once, my friend Eileen and me were coming along the field. Doreen and my sister was coming behind us. You've always got this great big stick in your hand when you go down hopping. All of a sudden we saw this bee, buzzing, and he went down this hole. So we said, "Oh I wonder what he's doing down there". We got this stick and poked it down this hole. We're going, "Can you hear that buzzing?" We saw one come out and then another, and we went "Quick, run!" So we run. Of course our two sisters are behind us, two years younger than us, and they're running, but we looked back and saw a great big black swarm of bees. We run into the square and our other cousin came out and they were stung all over. They had the doctors down and they was having nightmares. Now that was a terrible thing to bring on the children.
RICHIE: *All the men there was trying to suck the stings out of them.*

We think what we got up to was bad. But give me those days of terrible things rather than what they do today.

## Bookie's runner

The only rich person in our road was the man that my father worked for as a bookie's runner.
*Did you know that your dad was working as a bookie's runner?*
Oh yes! I didn't realise it was illegal. I realised he would get in trouble with the coppers if he was caught, but those days I didn't know of things being done illegally. He used to stand outside my friend's house. The door was always open and he would stand by her door. The men would go by and pass him a paper with sixpence inside, or they would throw it and he'd stoop down. His back was in the doorway and his eyes were looking all the time. Then he'd say to one of them, "Don't give me nothing. Don't pass anything. Is somebody coming down?" He would watch this person and if he didn't like the look of them, or didn't recognise them, he would go into my friend's house and shut the door. We'd be

at the door to tell him when they'd gone. The milkman could be a detective, dressed up as the milkman. And my dad would say, "Hello, no Milky today", and in the house he would go, knowing it was a policeman come to catch him. You could go through my friend's house, onto the wall and walk right the way down to ours. He would get there, open up the front window, and look out.

*Was he ever caught?*

Yes, I can recall him caught once myself. Whether he was caught more or not I don't know. He spent one night inside. He used to bring all the money home, put it on the table and spread the papers out, and Mum and him used to sort it all out. Straighten all the bets out, count the money and then take them when it was clear up to the top and give it to him. That bookie was the only rich person that I knew in that street.

## Nearly evacuated

I remember Billy and I going off with our gas masks and little bag of clothes and a nice bag of sweets. We were sitting around our classroom for a long time, not knowing why we weren't going. It was almost compulsory for the children to go. We sat around a long time and, of course, in the meantime we'd eaten all the sweets! But for some reason we didn't go. We ended up coming back from school. We'd just sat there in our classroom with gas masks and everything, waiting. The school stayed open during the war but most of the time we were in the shelters or spent half day at home and half day at school.

## The shelters

If the siren went at lunch-time we'd be down the shelter. When we were at school we didn't have a shelter as such. I think we used to collect in the hall. But when we were at Bellingham the shelter was in the garden, same as Deptford.

There weren't too many raids when we were at school. They were usually at tea-time. Mum used to give us our tea and we just sat there waiting for it to go. The candles were all down the shelter. Of course, there were quite a lot of us in there too! It was horrible, half-buried in the garden with concrete, then with a corrugated roof. There'd be a mattress on the floor. You can guess what that was like in the winter, straight on a concrete floor. There were so many of us that there were planks of wood going across with a mattress on and all the little ones would be up there. In the winter we had flowerpots round the inside with candles in and another flowerpot over the top. They got hot and also shone a light. A bit of a black smoke came through the hole at the top. There were so many of us, we snuggled together and kept warm.

*Was it damp in there?*

I don't recall it as being damp at the time, but thinking back it must have been. But we stayed indoors a lot, we didn't like going down there much. There was times, especially when we were eating, when we didn't bother going down the shelter. But my mother wanted you down there. My brother would be the last one, checking we were all in. My mother would be going "Shut that door" which was just a big bit of wood. I think we felt safe down there, I don't know why because a bomb's only got to touch that and you're gone. But at least you wouldn't have had the house coming down on top of you.

## Bombed out and homeless

We got bombed out with a very bad blast. They bombed the other side of the road and the house got it. Everything went. We were in the shelter out the back and we heard it go. Dad and Aunt Cag got out and went to look. They went through the house and didn't realise the damage. When we went upstairs to our flat everything was just bashed about. We didn't take a thing. They told us not to go in the house because it could all fall down. It was blasted so it had no windows. The furniture was all thrown everywhere, dust and dirt all over, things torn and pictures off the wall.

*You must have been upset?*
As a child I don't think you realised. I suppose my mother did. The only time I was upset was when I visited a friend and she was wearing my coat that was left there and they had our dining room table and chairs. That upset me because she said that my father said they could have them. Everything my mother had was taken. We had nothing. As we stood up, that's what we had.

We moved out that day and went up to the school: the whole family, my grandmother, my aunt that was single at the time and my cousin Sophie, mother and father and the six children. We went to the school and then we walked around, God knows where, people putting us up here, there and everywhere. We queued up for some old clothes at the school to re-rig us all out. They were all from the Salvation Army or something like that. There was a lot of us in that school, the hall was full of beds.

You had to go out during the day, walking around. We went to an aunt's first of all, up at Tanners Hill. They couldn't put us up because she had about six children of her own. One of ours had got a cough and my auntie thought it was whooping cough. She wanted to protect her children so we could only stay there one night.

I don't remember where nanny went. There are so many things that I can't remember. We went over to Downham to another uncle whose family was away evacuated. But they were coming home so then he said we'd got to go. I suppose we got evacuated straight away because I can't remember much after that.

## The evacuation

We were in a big rectory house in Mary Tavy, about $4^1/_2$ miles from Tavistock. Mother wouldn't let us go anywhere on our own then. Dad had to stay and work.

There was about 11 families in that house. Behind it there was a little chapel and there was a family living in the chapel as well. It was a lovely old house. There was three families eating and living in one room. There was a big table for all of us, another for a mother with two children and another with a couple of children. It had a big hall and great wide stairway and upstairs there were all these other rooms. We had our own bedroom, my mother and the children all in one. Every family had a bedroom but we shared the big kitchen with an old fire stove.

It had grounds all round. We started up little allotments, all us children. We used to walk down the hill in the mornings to get the fresh milk from the farmer. It was warm sometimes, beautiful. Up the road to another farmer to collect all the eggs that the chickens had laid in the hedges. See a chicken run, ooh, that was it, we ran to see where he'd laid his egg, and that went home to Mum. You were always hoping to see chickens run out of the hedges.

You didn't see a lot of people. Down the hill there was one farm, Friendly Farm I think it was called. Then you went right up the lane to another farm, and further up you came to the river. There wasn't many houses there.

The school that we went to was just one big hall. Some of us were only five, my brother was about 11, but we was all in one room. They weren't too friendly at the time, the children. They didn't really want evacuees but I think we outnumbered them in the end. But there was no violence or anything like that, and we weren't there long, only three or four months.

The only time I ever saw the sky red, was when we was in Devon. I think they had bombed Plymouth. We all went out. The sky was red and they said, "Oh they've got Plymouth tonight". We listened to Churchill, telling us all about the news and that.

## A new home but no dad

We came back because my father got us a council house in Bellingham as a home to come back to, but then he applied to go in the army on the Wednesday before we came back. We never really knew why he signed up. We always thought he could have got out of it because of his job, he was a riveter, and his age, he was the eldest man in the army.

*For a lot of men the war must have been a half-welcome escape?*

It's either that or it's "I want to be one of the boys". Dad was like that.

So we came back on the Sunday to this house and stuff that his sister had bought us from the Gratuity Money, the Bombed-Out Money, about £68 I think it was in all. His sister got us what she could find and that's what Mum come home to. It was very basic. Mum sat down and cried when she looked round the house. Our dining room seats were so old and worn the bulge went the wrong way, so we had to sit on the ridge of the seat. She couldn't get new stuff with that money. Second-hand everything, cups and saucers with cracks and chips.

Even though we were poor we had our pride and principles, and to drink out of cracked cups was bad. But during the war you were lucky to have cups. You were sometimes drinking out of small jam jars. Saucepans you couldn't get because they collected those to melt down. Second-hand beds and blankets and sheets, everything.

### Keeping in touch

Bellingham was a very nice estate but I missed Deptford. I missed my auntie that used to live with my grandmother. I grew up with her. She took me over when I was a baby. I used to sleep downstairs with her and grandmother more than in my own bed upstairs. I missed her a lot.

I missed my friends, Eileen and Joan and Rene. I only had three friends. Because you didn't leave your road, the kids in the street were your friends.

I went to Deptford regularly. Aunt and Gran lived next door to one another in Prince Street, and a couple of other aunts were round there. I used to visit my friends in Blackhorse Road and take a couple of sisters with me each time I went down. All the neighbours were thrilled to see us, the youngsters growing up and all that. When we all started courting, we lost touch of the friends but we used to still go down on Saturdays to see my grandmother and that went on and on and on, until she died. Deptford was a Saturday routine for my mother. A couple of the sisters used to go down to the High Street, take pie and mash back, a jar of liquor, and jam donuts from the shops.

We would get the bus. Once my father was in the army Mum wasn't so hard up anymore. She got more money then than when he used to work. She did quite nicely while he was away. We renewed all the furniture. Everything was thrown out and burnt in the garden. It was all new when Dad come home. Plus a couple of hundred in the bank. He spent that very quickly though; he said it was his.

My grandmother would walk if she had no money. She'd walk from Deptford to Bellingham. I often used to see Gran coming up the road and I'd run down and meet her. She was a dear old soul, sweating hot, tired out. She'd be saying "I've walked all the way, you know". She didn't have the money but she missed us so much.

### Bellingham Estate

The estate was built in the 1920s. Bellingham was different to Deptford. We had nice neighbours, but they had two children or just one child, very nicely off, thank you very much. Next door we had a quite resp-ected type of family, with about five grown-up children. They get a family come from Deptford with six children living next door and they must have thought "what have we got here?".

We were accepted after a little while. I don't remember how long it took. My friend lived next door and we did an awful lot during the war together. There was quite a posh lady across the road with one son. Her husband was in print. Every Christmas, we would get a stack of annuals from her husband's print. In the end they saw that my mum was on her own and they did all they could to help.

They used to tell Mum that we was

the best family up there. We never cheated. We wasn't allowed to cheat on our neighbours. We could cheat each other, but never the neighbours. Always help them out if you could, which we did.

When the raids was on they'd come round to check on 'White and the children'. They never called my mum Rose, always White. They would stand at the fence and see us all get down: "You alright, White?" "Yeah, we're alright", because there was no man there and six kids. They made sure we was down our shelter before they jumped into their own.

## Games of all sorts

We used to play one that they play now. Scissors, paper and stone. Fist is a stone, hand spread is paper, and two fingers sideways is scissors. The other game was a strip of wood about four inches long shaped at both ends like pencil ends. We used to put it on the kerb and all the kids would get another stick and you just hit it and whoever catches it, it's their turn.

We would play with our skipping rope, a long thick rope, from one side of the street to the other. This is the whole width of the street, because there was no cars around, apart from horse and carts. You would run along and catch the children running away, catch them in the rope, and tie them in that rope, and then they'd run with you until all the children were in the rope. The last two not caught would take the rope the next time.

We also had juggling against the wall and the poor lady down the end got it all the time cos hers was the only wall we could do it on. You would have a row of you. The first one throws it up the wall and as it bounces they jump over it and the next one catches it. The first one goes around to the back. The next one throws it, jumps over it and goes to the back. Also handstands up the wall, with your dress tucked in your knickers, of course.

For one game, you'd split the children up into two lots. Of one lot, the first would lean against the wall, standing up. Another one would come behind and hold onto his waist and he'd bend over, until you had a row of them, all up against that wall. Then the other lot, the first one come up running, jump on that first back and keep jumping, up, up, up, until he'd made room for all his mates, until they were all on. Now that lot have got to stand up and you start singing "1, 2, 3, all over, all over". Now if they fall down, that are holding you, they've got to do it again, you've got to jump again. If they're still standing up, holding on to you, the next lot bend over and have a go. It's like leapfrog.

We played all sorts with cigarette cards. You stood them up against the wall and then I'd have a bag of cards and flick them up the wall. All those I knock down, I keep. Another game, you just lay them there and you flick the other cards, and you've got to land on them. All you land on you can keep. I've still got a tin of our cards up in the loft. We had a big thick annual and say I put one in that page and three in that page, and five in that page, put some through the book, and close it up. Then Richie would come along and say "I'll give you five cards for five goes" or whatever. He would open it up five times trying to find the cards. He could come home with 20 cards but the craftier ones didn't put them in at all, of course.

We had marbles in the gutter with all the filth and we also cut our shoe boxes into arches and numbered them. Then I would roll the marbles up, and if I'd got them in number 3, you would have to give me three marbles.

We used to swap comics. The state of them! They had gone round and round, all torn and split and dirty, you know, but if you hadn't seen it, God that was a treasure. I don't think we ever had a comic bought for us. Probably the richer ones had a comic bought for them, or they went and bought one, because they had pocket money and we didn't. Then somebody would be kind enough and give us a bundle one day.

We sat on the pavement all day long in summer. You had no garden, only a backyard, so you were in the street.

# Entertainment

There was a big open-back lorry that used to come round with a roundabout on it. If you were lucky enough you had a jam jar. If you didn't have a jam jar it was a ha'penny. Well, a ha'penny for us kids would have been too much for our mother, so we had to make sure we found a jam jar per ride. We used to climb up on the lorry, sit in the little seat and it would go round, inside this open lorry.

You could give the rag and bone man a jam jar instead of money for something he was selling. He would either swap a jam jar or two or he'd say "Oh no, I want more than one jam jar". That was like bartering. He would get money on that jam jar down Robinson's jam factory.

We had a Scots band down, probably every year. They terrified me. I used to hide under the table. Gran didn't like them very much. She said, "Quick, under there, under there", and under the table we would go, like we did when it was thunder and lightning. We'd hear this bagpipe and look out the window, and there they would come, marching from the main road down into our street, blowing their bagpipes. For some reason I was frightened. The sound, I suppose, or maybe it was them dressed up.

The monkey man and the organ grinder used to come down. And you would get tradesmen, mostly Indian, selling rugs out of their cases. The only other foreign person in England that we knew of when I was young was the Italian man with the ice cream and his little push barrow. He had all these little bits of chopped up lemon in his ice creams. "Can we have a bit of lemon?" If you didn't get lemon in it, it wasn't right.

We had jesters come down and dance along the road, perhaps once a year. The other big thing was when the wood firms across the canal had their day's outing, their beano. They saved all their pennies and as they're setting off, we're all saying, "ta ta, ta ta", and out the window come all the pennies and ha'pennies. We would run and pick them up. We didn't have it for very long, though.

RICHIE: Dad said, "I'll look after that".

I remember hanging on the tail boards of the lorries going down Blackhorse Road, until you fell off. We used to wait for them to start off and then we would grab hold quick. Then as soon as they started picking up speed we'd let go and jump off. Eileen's sister Doreen was smaller. One time she was with us, all hanging on there, and we said "Right, jump!" So we all jumped off. She said "I can't, I can't", and she's gone right down Blackhorse Road. The lorry picked up speed, and she fell off on to the cobbled roads. The state of her! She was grazed all over.

*What about days out?*

Greenwich Park was our treat, mainly on Bank Holidays. Sit in the park, take your own drink and sandwiches. Now that was walking! Must be four miles from Blackhorse Road to Greenwich. We would all walk: my mother with a pram, with two inside, and three or four of us tiny tots walking, and my father strolling along beside us.

The only other treat was Dad taking me to Blackheath where his sisters lived. I must have been only tiny, cos I remember him carrying me when I was tired. They gave me half a crown but he wouldn't give it to me. Dad used to look after that. I think that's all we went for. Cos he used to like his little drink.

We would go just to Deptford Park by ourselves. Mum used to bring us round bread and jam, a bottle of lemonade. We never had a holiday at all. Not many people did in those days. You weren't envious, because nobody did that sort of thing. Hopping was the holiday.

## Shows in the garden

Our street and the next street would get all the kids round and dress up and put on our own little show, tap dancing, pantomines and all sorts. I think we used to charge them a ha'penny or a penny to come in the back gate. At the time my mother had just had our last sister and she used to get these bottles of strong concentrated orange free from the welfare. So we'd make pints of orange and sell it to all these kids in the garden. We used to practice this step dancing and a bit of ballet. I would do a pantomine and get lots of people to act a little bit. It was just walking around the garden dressed up. We had jumble sales as well. We would make little brooches and hair slides. We sent some money once to the Red Cross, during the war, me and Vera next door. It was only about 12/ 6 but we got a letter thanking us for it.

We used to play shoe shops. We would write up shoe sizes up on the bricks and we had a ladder to climb up and get the shoes. Couldn't get nothing down. Just pretend it was size 6, and play all day like that. No rows, no fights. Hardly ever a fight went on. One of my friends used to pick on Sylvie quite a bit. They clashed and I would have to sort her out. Not with fighting, but going up and telling her off. Other than that we were pretty good and there was a good atmosphere.

## Strange substances

A friend and I used go out for the old girls to get their shopping. You got these little packets of snuff, in a bit of newspaper. We would try it out before we got back. We were sneezing until we got there. These old ladies had all brown round their noses, and we always used to wonder why. It was their snuff.

I remember going to the bottom of the road and round the corner to the arches. There was a little place there where we could buy pet food. It was like slices of beef and we would eat a slice between us before we came home. It was horse's flesh. That's terrible, ain't it? We never had beef, you see, when we were little.

## Food and housework

We were OK because there was a lot of us, so it went round. Also if my mother couldn't afford it, she didn't use it all. Mum didn't need all the jars of jam you could have so she'd swap with somebody that would enjoy a jar of jam. She couldn't afford bacon so if somebody bought her a pound of bacon they would go home with sweets. My mother did very well with cooking. We never starved. The only thing we did use up was the eggs. Nobody could cut one in half as clever as my mother. Fried or boiled, she had to share one egg between two of us on toast.

We didn't go hungry but we neverr used to eat a lot of fancy stuff. They couldn't afford it. It was meat Mum missed most of all. I remember during the war making bacon roly poly every week, and I hated it.

RICHIE: *If you looked at Mum's hands, you would think she was a cripple, because her knuckles were twisted through scrubbing that board.*

Well, I used to do that, I used to enjoy doing that. I would stay home from school on a Monday, when Mum was doing the washing. I did a lot of the cooking and housework with her. She didn't ask me to do it, I loved housework. I enjoyed helping her. She was a mum to help. The eldest ones did it. As the younger ones grew up, then life changed. I started really quite young in babysitting and things like that. Cos my father was in the forces, and when he came home, they would go to the top of the road for a drink, and I'd be there with all these kids, when I was 11. It's not allowed today but there was other children doing the same thing.

## The facts of life

I tell you what I couldn't understand in the war. Why my mother always went to the front of the queue when we were queueing up for oranges or bananas, or hot cross buns during the war. It was because she was pregnant.

*You didn't realise she was pregnant?*

No, I didn't know. She had my sister when I was 14. I didn't really know she was pregnant, I just thought she was getting a bit big. I didn't know the facts of life at all. She never told us nothing. She was embarassed. She couldn't talk to us about it.

## Burning shoes

We had no central heating, of course, in those days. If we had nothing, no money, no coal, then Dad used to say, "You got any old shoes?" We would all go upstairs and sort our old shoes out. They were all leather in those days. There would be a bucket full of dust in the coal cellar and he'd damp that down and then line the fire with paper and a little bit of wood. He would stack all our shoes tightly together over it. He'd get the wet coal dust and pat it down tight, and set it alight. My God, that was warm! It all stayed in a square block, old burning shoes. We had a beautiful fire that would last a good half a day.

RICHIE: *Our hot water bottles were brick. You put them on metal hobs and they would get hotted up. We got one blanket per bed and the rest was overcoats. The girls would sit and knit patchwork quilts. It was all self-preservation really. Every penny we earned went back to Mum.*

We took very little. All we ever spent in those days, was on clothes and once or twice a week to the pictures.

On Saturdays a couple of us would go shopping with Mum, and a couple would stay at home and do the top to bottom. We worked very well. No pocket money. The only pocket money we had was Mum bringing us sweets in or taking us to the pictures every now and again. Maybe that's the trouble of today, they get too much pocket money. Our generation have started that. Because we had nothing we didn't want them to have nothing. You got better yourself, the house was better, more equipped, so it was an easier life. And women started going out to work, of course.

*When you were that age were you very conscious of being poor?*

No. Everyone around us was the same. Joanie and Reenie's dad had a good job. Their mother was a great friend of my mum and she used to pass all their clothes on to me and my sister. We thought they were rich. They probably weren't, but she gave us her left-offs and my mother accepted them.

## The pawnbrokers

The most humiliating experience was on a Monday, going up the pawnshop with our new coats and hats, and perhaps Dad's new pair of shoes or his suit, if he had one at the time. Our best coats went in on a Monday and out on a Friday, so we could have them for Sundays.

My mother used to go to Deptford quite a lot to see my gran in the evenings. She would take her dinners and bags of coal. But I think it might have been also to go to the pawnshop. She didn't have to go so much after Dad was in the army. I remember the Catford one closing down and I don't remember her going very far or very much after that.

RICHIE: *As a kid I couldn't understand why Mum used to go out with a parcel one day and at the end of the week come home with one. You just didn't realise.*

Before I was nine I realised about it and I used to go up there on my own or with my mother or grandmother. It was just at the top of Blackhorse Road, round to the right and the next turning.

*Did you feel humiliated at the time, or is that just looking back?*

No, no, then.

*So not everybody did it?*

No, not everybody did it. My new coat went into that pawn shop, but theirs didn't. Their father probably didn't drink like my father drunk. His money came home for food, but my father's didn't always come home. Half of his went in the beer.

*Did you realise at the time that was where the money was going?*

Oh yes, we knew Dad would always be in the pub. We learnt that very young. At the weekends we would be playing outside the pub. Then on a Monday we've got no money for dinner. So Gran would feed us. She fed us more during the week than Dad did.

Mum used to mend all our shoes. Dad sent his home from Belgium. She would mend them and send them back again. I think he even had the cheek to send this other Belgian fella's shoes home, someone he had palled up with. He had palled up with a family there and went into their home. My mum used to send food to them, cos Belgium had been occupied. Mum had cheese and bacon from our rations and sent it off to Belgium. By the time it got there, the cheese was green, Dad said, but they just used to cut it all off. The bacon was a bit smelly, but they used to lay it in boiled water and it was fine.

## Schooling and work

My education suffered terribly. Good God, I had no education! I don't remember much early schooling. I got the cane in Deptford Park School because I had my sums wrong. I had the same teacher as my mum had when she was young. She gave Mum all her sewing, patching her husband's pants and his underclothes and darning his socks. Then we went to Evelyn Street School. They made us go to sleep in the afternoon on little fold-out beds. I hated that.

We went to Devon and we had hardly any education there at all. It was three months and we lost quite a lot. When we went to Bellingham, there was only half a day education.

I found it hard to read, hard to spell, hard for maths. All I was good at was needlework, cooking, writing. I used to love writing, but in those days we had no books to write in so we had to save all the old books and write in between the lines of what was already written. We had to cross out all the old lines, use them all up again. We couldn't afford hymn books so I would stay in rather than going out to play and the teacher would get me to write out hymn books.

I found reading really hard. You had to stand up and they said "Oh you, read that paragraph." It would come to my turn and I would stand up but I couldn't get it out. No way.

*RICHIE: Rosie, I was the same. I didn't learn to read until I had left school.*

That's right. But what did the teacher do? She says, "Oh Rosie, teatime dear", or in the morning it would be, "Oh coffee, Rosie". I was the girl that made all the teachers' coffees in the morning and teas in the afternoon. I was teacher's pet so I got away with not doing my lessons. If it was cookery and my mother couldn't afford it that day the teachers would buy my cookings from me, rather than me not doing it.

I thoroughly enjoyed school. I stayed on another six months because I didn't want to leave. But I was a dunce. I was about third from the bottom right through schooling. When I left at 14½ I started reading by myself. I didn't resent it but I do think it would have been better if they had realised I was dyslexic or whatever. But they didn't in those days. There was a lot of girls as bad as me, I wasn't the only one. You got the bright sparks that were up top, then me and a handful more down at the bottom.

They didn't have so many open days in those times so the mother didn't really know very much. With my father being away in the army, no-one was aware of what was happening.

When I left school and wanted to take up dressmaking, Dad wouldn't let me travel to London. My friend went and she ended up making all my bridesmaids' clothes and my bride's dress. I could have been doing that myself but he wouldn't let me go. "No, don't let her travel. Think of the bombs, think of the fog, trains, this, that and the other." So that was that. Then I wanted to do hairdressing but that wasn't enough money. My friend went to work in a factory cos it was good money. But Dad says "No. Don't you let her go in a factory. You put her in a shop." So I ended up in a dry cleaners in Bellingham. But then I went to the plastic factory where they made plastic mouldings, cups, saucers, plates, sweet jar lids. That was without Dad knowing because he was in Belgium. There was plenty of jobs going. You could start a job today, leave it tonight and start another tomorrow morning. Then the war ended and he was coming home, so I had to leave the factory.

So I quickly got to Woolworths at Catford. I was earning 25 shillings a week then. I was there for about six months, but I didn't like it there, the manager was weird. I said "I want to leave tomorrow". "You can't, you've got to put a week's notice in." So I went and told Dad and he went to the manager. I don't know what happened in that office but he come to the counter and said to me "Come on, girl. Home." That was that. I said "Where can I work now?" "Well where do you want to go?" "You wouldn't let me go with Betty, you wouldn't let me go there or there. I want to go to the factory in Sydenham and earn all this money, like my other friends." So he let me go and I was there until I got married when I was 26.

## VE Day

Our house and next door had the alleyways, so you had a sort of round arch between, and you went through to the back gardens. Over the gate we wrote up VE DAY and VICTORY and WELCOME HOME, DAD and put up all the flags. We had a lovely party. One of my aunts and her four daughters and friends came up from Deptford and had their party with us in our road. Our fire burned a big hole in the corner of the street. All the wooden garden gates went on the fire. In the morning when it all died down, the tar road had melted and we had a great big crater. The council came along and repaired the road. Nothing was said. Everybody was happy. The war was over, what was there to complain about?

We had roast potatoes and a girl brought her piano right out and played on her steps. It went on until the early hours of the morning. It was lovely. No more bombs, and Dad coming home.

## Welcome home Dad?

*How did you feel about that coming home?*
Dad coming home? Oh well, it was all lovely, wasn't it? Very nice.
*Did it turn out easy to get used to him being around again?*
Not very easy no.
*And why not?*
Well....

*RICHIE: You've got to tell him. I've been honest.*
Yeah, but it's not nice, is it?
*RICHIE: But it's the truth, Rosie.*
Well, Dad was a man's man, and he liked his drink. They all did in those days. He loved the company of his mates. So Mum was Mum and her place was in the home with the kids. That's how her life was. When we were in the war, we had a nice closeness, no arguments or nothing. We were a simple living family that didn't ask for much and we were always laughing.

When Dad come home, Mum had saved up this money. He said that was his money. I think he bought Mum a coat out of it but then he would have his nights up at the top. He would expect her to go with him but she didn't always want to go to the pub, and with the children, she couldn't. She saw this money she had saved over four years being spent in the pub. If she had known, she could have spent it before he come home and got things that she wanted.

Anyway, he was a little bit violent years ago when we was small. He tried his weight when he came home from the army and he couldn't get away with it, because we'd grown up and we weren't going to see Mum hurt anymore. We stood up for her and, of course, that didn't please Dad very much so there was a bit of a disturbance now and again. I think he felt that it was one-sided. We all thought a lot of Mum and not him. But it was of his own doing. He was a silly man. He'd been protective with us all his life, didn't want to see us hurt. I'll give him his due there, but he did all the things that he wouldn't let us do.

*RICHIE: Maybe he would have got away with it longer if it hadn't been for the war.*
Oh yes, and we would probably have left home by then. But while the war was on, we had some good years with our mother. Mum had got used to doing things differently. She had neighbours and they would pop in, not a lot, but they were nice ones over there. When he came home he started objecting to them coming in, objecting if they called out or

come round. He didn't want her to go round there, didn't want them to come here. He wanted her to be in all the time.

He used to get annoyed with Richie. Dad would go up for a drink and Richie would have his mates playing cards, no money or anything, around the table. He'd have had his couple of drinks and he would come in and stop it. He didn't like you playing cards in the house.

The pub was my father's field really. That was his relaxation, that was where he enjoyed being. I always remember one time that I said "Dad, you know they're only playing cards" but he went "I don't want them playing cards in my house". All the mates used to trot off home, and me being the eldest one, I would have a go at him. I was always rowing with him. It did alter our lives quite a lot.

*At the end of the war were you at courting age, or were you too young?*

No, my father wouldn't have allowed that, cos I was about 15 or 16. You weren't allowed boyfriends at 16. I wasn't allowed make-up. I wasn't allowed to go dancing. I wasn't allowed to go swimming. I wasn't allowed to have a bike. I was 19 before I could have a bike. My friends had bikes but he was over protective. He could see danger all the time. Evidently when he was young he had a bike but he nearly went under a bus. I was nearly 21 before I was allowed to go on a holiday. I was courting my husband Ray just before I was 21. He was over protective. It stopped a lot of your pleasure, compared to what children are doing today. On the other hand, we all grew up closer and didn't argue the toss. We accepted it, couldn't do much else but accept what he said.

*The war must have been quite nice in that respect, because you didn't have that all the time?*

Yes, it's a shame to say that, but I think it is true.

RICHIE: *We got more visits from our aunts and we used to visit them more.*

He wouldn't allow anybody in the house if he could help it. If Mum stayed at the door too long, talking to the insurance man, or someone like that, he would be out there wanting to know what's going on. He was very possessive where Mum was concerned.

**Changing times**

*Did the atmospere change after the war?*

I would say it took about five or six years. People started getting cars and televisions and then people were moving out and new neighbours moving in, and nobody was friendly anymore. They didn't know you. They didn't have all that worry from the bombing or the closeness any more.

The new neighbours were never as friendly. They didn't want to know. They were a very close couple and they stayed on their own. That was a shame because a whole batch of us were friends. As people moved away, it altered. "My home's better than yours" and all that started. It was a better world to live in, when the war was on.

# RICHIE

## sixpence for mum

Like many of the Welches, Richie was born in the family home at 48 Blackhorse Road, Deptford, in 1936.

He remembers fishing for tiddlers in the nearby Surrey Canal as a tiny infant and seeing the sky lit red when the docks were being bombed in 1940.

When the family was bombed out it was hard to find space for mum and six children, so they were evacuated to Devon. After a few months they returned and moved on to the 1920s cottage estate at Bellingham.

Richie's father, Bill White, was a bookie's runner in the 1930s and was a well known local character. His mother, Rose Welch, was "the type who was always there, a diamond, never out, never missing".

Dad knew everybody in the street. When the Old Bill come along he could go in any door, run right along the back wall and be sitting indoors as though nothing had happened when they knocked on the door. I've got a court order from 1938, when he had to appear at Greenwich Magistrates' Court on bail of ten pounds for taking bets.

He was a fantastic darts player. People reckon he was probably the best darts player in Deptford, Greenwich, Bermondsey. He used to work on the darts stall at the fairground in Deptford High Street. Before he was married, he made plenty of money, obviously doing a bit of fiddling on the side. He told me that he had one of these old wind-up gramophones stacked up with half crowns and two shilling pieces. He was going to buy a fairground or an amusement arcade down in Southend. He told his dad what he was going to do and his dad said "Where d'you get the money?"

"Well I've been working for it."

"You ain't effing leaving home. You're staying here. This is where you live and this is where you're staying." So he couldn't go.

His father was a very hard man. That was the White side. He worked for Val de Travers the roadbuilders. I've got a photo of him out in South America, Buenos Aires I think, with a big white Stetson and a gun. If you looked at the people that he's with in the photo, you'd think "Christ, lock them up!" He went out there to show them how to build roads. He knew his stuff, but a hard man. My father took on from that.

Mum done sewing as a young woman but after she got married she had no time for work with eight kids. I was the fifth. The third, Lenny, died when he was about two. They just took him in hospital and my father always swore blind that the hospital let him die. He was sick but if children went in the hospital them days, the chance of them coming out was really remote. I don't think they ever really knew what he died of. Each of us, as our turn come along, looked after each other. As each come along they all took their turns.

We had other relations up Blackhorse Road. Our cousin Kitty was born in our house. Other Welch cousins lived up the road and my Nan's brothers lived there too. There was quite a lot of in and out of each other's houses. They all knew each other, most of them worked on the docks.

I've been back to Blackhorse Road but all the houses are gone now.

## Disappearing Dad

When the war started Dad was working as a riveter at Frederick Braby's, the iron galvanising place on the canal. He didn't have to join up because building barges was war work. They gave him a choice but he signed up to the Royal Army Service Corps and my mum swore it was to get away from all us kids!

He disappeared in about 1940. I can remember him being there when we were bombed out of Blackhorse Road. I would imagine we were bombed out when they bombed the docks, because I can remember as a child coming out of our house and looking up and all the sky was red. That's my earliest memory of the war. The house wasn't flattened, it was more blasted, all the windows and that.

All I can remember is that afterwards we were walking round the streets, Mum with us children, just walking the streets virtually all night. One of my aunts took us in for one night but my sister Violet had a cough. She thought it was whooping cough and she thought it best if we didn't stay because she had six or seven children, you can understand. So we left there and had another night walking round in the dark. It always seemed to be dark. Nobody wanted to take us in, which was fair enough as they all had kids. We finished up in a great big school hall with hundreds of people, all in chaos. They only allowed us to stay one night because they thought Violet had whooping cough and they didn't want it to spread. They kicked us out the following morning. My Nan and Grandad White took us in for a very short period, a week at most, and then we were evacuated down to Devon.

## Evacuation

We were taken down to Mary Tavy near Tavistock but we were only there for about three or four months. I can remember fields and again a great big room with lots of people in it. There were quite a few people from Deptford down there living in the same big mansion with lots of grounds. It was pleasant. My eldest brother wanted to stay down there because he loved it, roaming the countryside. To us it was fresh.

The war was all around even down there. I remember lorries going along through the lanes with planes on the back of them. It always worried me whether I dreamt it but my brother remembers it too.

I loved it there. I can remember cows and sheep and chickens and going down to get milk, with stacks of kids. We used to walk down to the fields, climbing over what you would call a stile.

They weren't very nice to us down there though. My mum didn't like it so she took us home.

## School

I didn't go to school in Devon. I didn't go to school hardly at all during the war actually. There wasn't a lot of school about then. We spent more time on our local school roof than in the classroom. When we moved back we came to Bellingham and the school was just round the corner from us. It was a low single-storey building with a flat area on the roof and we used to play on there. If balls went up on the roof during the day we'd be up there every night of the week, collecting the balls and finding pens and pencils. The last thing we'd do would be to get to the middle bit where the school bell was. Before we got off we used to ring that bell, run along the roof, jump into the bushes, over the gate and we'd be sitting there when the old school caretaker came along. He never thought we could make it so quick.

We used to run along the ridge of the roof as kids. There was a flat bit on one side but the other side dropped right into the playground. You always thought "Well, if I fall down, I'll fall on the flat roof anyway". You never thought of falling the other way. I wouldn't do it now to save my life and I've done roofing. I'll always remember when Charlie's father come out and see us kids running across there. He called Charlie, and Charlie nearly fell off the roof. There was this six foot gate we used to throw ourselves over and Charlie's trying to get over it but his father's got a great big two inch leather belt and he's whacking at his fingers where they're peeking over.

When I did go to school, most times it was half a day, or if there was air raid warnings you just went under the table so you didn't get any schooling. Anybody that learned anything, to read, write or anything during the war was very, very fortunate because there weren't the teachers to go round. I found a report from school the other day from 1948 and there was 35 in the class and that's after the war. So you can imagine during the war there was probably 40, 45 or more. So although they had a register, if you wasn't there they didn't really worry. They sent someone round but what could they do?

I hated school, I didn't go for the last year but I went back for the last term. They said "What you doing here? You left last year." I said "No, I've been ill." "You're joking?" "No." So they put me in a class with just two or three of us, and that's how we spent our last term, sitting in a classroom larking about all day. My entire schooling would amount to about three or four years.

I could barely read when I left. When I was about 14 I learnt a bit because I needed to. Mind you, that report I've got says I came sixth in the class so imagine what the rest of them was like! I think most of mine I learnt at home not at school. I just couldn't concentrate at school. They used to say "Get up and read, White". I'd get up and just stand there like a lemon. I couldn't open my mouth because I couldn't read. All my learning and all my knowledge is what I've got since I left school. My mum couldn't read or write until my dad went away and my brother used to do all the writing of letters. He said "Mum, you've got to learn to do this yourself" and he taught her to read and write during the war. I've got a copy of Nanny Welch's marriage certificate upstairs. It's got a cross and it says "This is the mark of Mary Ann Gard". That's all she could do, she couldn't read or write, just a cross for her signature.

### Sheltering

When we moved on to Bellingham we had an Anderson shelter in the back garden. It was half buried in the ground, made of cement with a corrugated iron roof and reinforced cement over the top. It was about six foot square inside with bunks, with just a little door probably about three foot by two foot to get into it. The few times we did use it it was very damp and full of spiders. There was no electric down there. You had to take a candle and your bedding down there each night. You couldn't leave it there because it would get damp or infested. If we did use it it would probably be in the summertime, but I wouldn't imagine us using it. If there was a raid we went straight under the table. Everybody had a big old table in them times and we all used to be under the table.

DICKIE: *Our favourite game as children was what they call 'Chicken' now. When the siren went there would be thousands of us kids and all the mothers used to be calling names and the last one to run away was the winner. You didn't fear it. Your mother at home would be worried and you would go: "What's wrong, Mum?" I can remember my old man coming home from Belgium. When he saw all tis going on, all the doodlebugs and that, he was scared out of his life.*

### Toys and games

You made your own toys. We used to make scooters. I don't know how we managed but we would get the ball bearings, the bits of wood and long bolts. Everybody had a scooter, or the old Go-Kart made with four pram wheels. That was easily come by. Opposite the school there was a water tank. The houses had been bombed and they'd built a big brick water tank on the bit of waste. That used to be the local dump and that's where you got the bits to make up your first bike.

We used to sit on this water tank, throwing stones at the school windows, criminal really! I was saying we weren't vandals, but we were really. It wasn't every night but just occasionally.

We used to collect shrapnel during the war. Every boy had a box of shrapnel and you'd go out hunting for little jagged bits of metal. They were your pride and joy but I'm sure my mother took mine down to Wilson's to be sold one day when I was at school!

All the old type games. I can remember knocking down ginger, knocking at people's doors and running off. That was the natural one, but also marbles. The girls used to have a big bit of rope from one side of the road to the other with two or three turning it and about ten or twelve kids in the middle, all skipping. The rope was right across the road but you'd never see cars about then. If a car did come along it would see you and go round the other way. They'd never stop you.

Our favourite game as children was what they call 'Chicken' now. When the siren went there would be crowds of us kids and all the mothers used to be calling names and the last one to run away was the winner. You didn't fear it. Your mother at home would be worried and you would go: "What's wrong, Mum?" I can remember my old man coming home from Belgium. When he saw all this going on, all the doodlebugs and that, he was scared out of his life.

When we were at Blackhorse Road we used to play round the canal. I don't think we was allowed to. That was the sort of thing that you did because it was there. When we moved to Bellingham we used to go wandering off a lot because just along from there was the countryside.

## Beckenham Place Park

They had a camp on there for Italian prisoners of war. We used to go over there and lie on the hill and watch them in the camp. They were let out sometimes and they used to walk round the estate. People would take them in and give them tea and biscuits.

We used to go bird's nesting in the park. That's illegal now but I had a beautiful collection of bird's eggs. You knew every bird by the eggs. For a child it was a good time because there was no law and order, no park-keepers as such and the woods were dense like a forest. I remember pushing a way through it and getting lost. There were probably a dozen kids used to go down there together. Everyone in the street had big families.

We used to lie in the woods, in the thick bushes down there. They used to play golf. It was a rich man's game then, and whenever a golf ball came near we'd nick it. We'd take it to this big house nearby where there was a kind of cleaning machine. You pedalled with your foot and these brushes cleaned the ball for you. We would sell them for sixpence or a shilling for a good ball. We earned quite a lot of money. It was notorious down there for us kids, but they couldn't catch us. After the war they thinned out the bushes.

As little as we were we probably shouldn't have been there. It was a really rich area and the gardens used to run two hundred foot right down to the park. A lot of them were abandoned. I suppose the rich people thought "right, we'll get out" and they just left them.

We used to play in the bombed-out houses and I think now of how dangerous it could have been. Some had no roof if they had been bombed or blasted out and they were open to the elements.

---

**You wanted to try and get some money to help your mum, not like now when the kids go out nicking for themselves.**

---

On one trip to Beckenham there were four of us. I don't know how but we knew lead or metal was worth money, so we went up on the roof of a bombed-out house. We got a big box out of the shed and we filled it with lead – square bits of flat lead. We carried it home and as we got into the turning, Peter's brother Bobby come out and said "What you got there?" He went "Lead", and his brother belted him and said "You get in, you'll get nicked, you'll get put away". So he disappeared and then Reggie, David's big brother, heard and gave him a whack and made him go in. So that left me and Charlie. We were panicking a bit, thinking "what's this?" and we had this big box of lead. When we got to Charlie's house he didn't want to know, he was worried. So I dragged it down to my house. I took it in and my mum said "What you got there?"

"I got some lead, Mum."

"You little bugger, where'd you get that?"

"Off the roof."

"You could have killed yourself."

We put it on a push chair, rags on top, and took it to Wilson's, the scrap metal dealer down at Lower Sydenham. We got four pounds which was a lot of money. Wilson never asked no questions. I went to Charlie and I said "We got two pounds". So I gave him a pound and me and my mum had three. That must have lasted us for ever, three pounds, dear, oh dear! We never went back for more though. We were scared after that.

**Scheming**

I don't know why but we was always scheming. There was no TV, nothing to do, so you just got up to mischief.

Robinson's Jam Factory was just down the road from us and all the local girls worked in Robinson's Jam Factory. They used to give you ha'penny back on the jam jars, so we went round knocking on all the houses in Bromley and Beckenham: "Have you got any jam jars?" That's how you got your money for Saturday morning pictures. Ha'penny on the jam jar or tuppence or thruppence on lemonade bottles or beer bottles. We used to go round with a shovel, a little brush and a barrow collecting horse manure. If you saw a horse you'd follow it for miles because all the local men that wasn't in the Army wanted the manure to put on their tomatoes or the garden. Many a time you'd pick it up and someone would rush out shouting "Get away from here, you don't live round here, that's ours!". Truthfully! "You get down your own street." They'd do their nut because you was poaching their horse manure. Really, I suppose we were toe-rags, but that was the way. It was fun.

It seemed as though we was always laughing. When the air raids come and the siren went, you just stayed on the corner. There'd probably be a dozen kids or more and your mother would be calling out, "Richie, Violet, David", and all that. You'd be standing there in the dark and the last one to go was the bravest. But your mother's going grey by this time, cos you could hear the planes coming over.

We used to watch the dogfights, both at home and down hopping. I saw a lot of them. That was part and parcel of the war. It was so exciting that you didn't think people was dying. It was like a film. You see the guns firing and they come so low. There were times when you could actually see men sitting in the cockpits. I can remember planes chasing after the doodlebugs, trying to shoot them out the skies or veer them away. Sometimes when you get older you think it's a dream but when we were down hopping, the planes come over and you'd see a pilot come along and try and tip the wing to divert them so they'd turn around and go back out to sea. It was a spectacular thing. They were so brave. Down at hopping you didn't see a lot of bombing because they used to go straight to London so you was virtually safe. They just went straight above your head.

**Hopping**

We always went hopping. We went to East Farleigh in Kent. That still had to go on during the war. It was your holiday. Not all the children round the street went. We was the only family, I think, that used to go. At the end of the six weeks school holidays they went back to school and we went down hopping for another four weeks. The schools didn't like it. They used to send round notices 'No hop picking'.

We used to catch the train hopping. When you arrived there was lots of walking to do. Sometimes you got a lift from the station but mostly you walked. The huts were just a brick building, not plastered or rendered up, just ordinary brick. One room, no toilet, no electric light. They had an apex roof but the walls between was only built up to the beginning of the apex so there was space above and we could climb up the wall, over the top and talk to our cousins in the next hut. There was just one long wooden bench. We used to take the mattresses down and fill them up with straw and lay it on there. The women, all the kids and then the men, all laid on that one big long bench. I remember earwigs and things like that.

The place was like an encampment with an entrance and the huts all built in a square so there was a compound inside. They used to have two or three open fires with a metal rod over to hang the pots and saucepans on. That's where all the cooking was done and all the hot water was got from. You'd do your own cooking but because there were so many of our relations down there, they'd have massive dinners, mostly stews and things like that. It was all done when you come home from a day. There was always a bucket of hot water. If you was the last it was green and black where everybody else had washed in it, all slimy – really it was so barbaric. The light was an oil light and it was all black up the wall where it had burnt, year in, year out.

I went back to see them about two years ago. There's only part of them standing. You look at them now and you think, "How on earth did we live in them for four weeks, year after year?"

I loved it. You got up early. As dawn broke you was virtually up and you had to get down the fields as near to seven as possible. Hops, they're like vines, they grow up to eight or ten foot in the air on wires. They're tied up at the top. You got your bin which is eight foot long maybe and you pulled the hop bine. First thing in the morning it was full of dew or if it had been raining it was full of mud. As you pulled the bine the dew used to go all over you and you'd be soaking wet. After a while your little hands used to go dark green and then virtually black. And the smell! You could never get rid of the smell of the hops. However little you were you had to help. Once you'd done a bit your mother used to say "Go on, then". We used to run away and go in the woods or go scrumping. You'd come back and have your dinner out in the field.

If it rained you didn't go out for the day, but if you didn't go out, you didn't get paid. It was really boring if you had a few days' rain. Although, having said that, there was always someone that would play a mouth organ or whatever. Down our place there was a man played a banjo and there used to be singing. Every night was like a gypsy festival, everybody singing songs. There'd be someone tap-dancing or they'd all be dancing. They was good times.

There would be the same people there every year. We was always in with our Nan, right in the corner and then next door to us was Aunt Priss and then Aunt Nance. Aunt Edie was in what they called the slates, a little bit further up the hill. There was stacks of cousins, so the kids didn't really get bored. They would do now if they didn't have their computers and their videos, but then there was always something to do, climb trees or something.

The farmers knew you brought cooking apples home. You had cooking apples right up till Christmas. It was part and parcel of coming home from hopping, you were spoiled. The last day they used to throw everything on the fire, packets of Bisto and things like that. At the weekends the men used to come down if they wasn't away in the army. During the war it was mostly the women and kids. There was a lot of men that never went in the war but it was mostly women. My father only went down a few times. He wasn't a hopping man really.

Come weekends I always used to go up the pub. The men would come down from London and I can remember being in the pub from as little as three or four, sitting outside at least, and they'd all come home singing. You can understand the locals not really liking them because they were singing at the tops of their voices and they'd get home and probably have a little bit of a party outside.

One time someone came in saying "Look at all these planes" and the sky seemed to be full of planes of all different sizes. British planes. Maybe they were going to D-Day or Dresden.

We saw the one that done Sandhurst School, shot all the children up there. My brother was in Catford that day and he said it was frightening. They come down just over the tops of the houses. They knew it was a school and they shot all them little children during their dinner break. We was so close to it on Bellingham,, we saw planes flying low but we didn't know what it was till the next day. Even as little kids you knew what was a German plane and what wasn't, and if you see them you ducked. You learnt from a young'un to duck.

## Blackouts

They say everybody had blackouts, but people had to buy their own blackout material and not everybody could afford it for all their windows. People were very poor. They would come round and call out "Number thirty-two! Cover that window, pull that curtain." I remember blankets going up, and anything to keep out light, nail it up there. What you've got to realise is that everything was very basic, no curtain tracks. It would be wires or string holding up your curtains. You didn't have no fancy swish rails. All the schools had sticky-in crosses on the windows in case of blasts and half way up there used to be sandbags so that the blast wouldn't go right in on all the children. Hospitals and most public buildings were like that, criss-cross with sticky tape.

We used to stay out on the street corners. You had to be in at a certain time but your parents were a little lenient. You stayed out until it was as dark as you could possibly get but you was too young to be out too late anyway.

## Half an egg and a bag of crackling

My mum was probably the best in our street at being able to cut open a soft boiled egg. She could cut it in half and turn it over, wouldn't spill a drop. We'd have half an egg. She used to buy sweets, a quarter of whatever, and she'd give us two each to go to school with. You had your ration books and for sweets they used to tear out the coupons, but on other things, fruit and meat, they used to put a cross with a coloured pencil. My mum used to rub that off with bread. Using bread as a rubber, would you believe! But you could always see it and I remember going in the butchers or the greengrocers, saying could I have so-and-so.

"Your mum's already had that."

"She hasn't."

"Yes she has."

"No, no, that ain't used."

"Oh, OK then", and they'd give you the little bit extra, but they knew.

You swapped the clothes coupon for food because you could do without clothes. The richer people would give you money for them, so you could go and buy. Because you couldn't afford things like that, not unless you went and got lead every week, of course!

My mother always tried to give us a bit of meat each day but it was very tiny. If she had a joint which she did on Sunday, that would always be a stew on the Monday. That was whatever was left over and dumplings, carrots and potatoes.

You had fish and chips now and again because that was quite a cheap meal. When we was kids we knew all the shop owners. You'd go in the fish shop and they'd give you a bag of crackling, the hard bits of fat or batter, just in little balls. In the baker's, you'd buy the stale cakes from the day before or a pound of broken biscuits because they were cheaper than the full ones.

You used to plant vegetables in your back garden, everybody did it. We had our own potatoes and lettuces and people had allotments. Everybody used to grow vegetables, as many as they could. If you had flowers they'd be in the front garden. Dig For Victory, that's my memory.

People used to share the vegetables and stuff. The Wigsalls next door were very good to us. Mr Wigsall was too old for the army. He worked in a butchers so he used to fetch us home a little bit of meat now and again, and he used to look after us. He was very good to my mum. We never had a radio but they used to let me go in and listen to Dick Barton, Snowy and Jock every night.

People also kept chickens for the eggs. Years ago chicken was a delicacy and if you were rich you'd have a chicken for Christmas dinner. We had them running wild in our back garden. They used to go through the fence to other people's gardens. We went down to see our Nan once when she lived in Prince Street, Deptford. Next door was an aunt who had two boys and they had chickens, and on top of the wall there was a roll of chicken wire. I asked whether they wanted it but they said they needed it, and they wouldn't let me have it. My Nan heard me.

"What's that, boy?"

"Well that chicken wire, I want it for my chickens."

"Oh yes."

Well, several weeks later she turned up at our door. She'd walked from Deptford to Bellingham with this roll of wire underneath her arm.

"There boy, I've got some wire for you."

She was a darling, she really was. All those years she used to visit everybody, she had no money, she just used to walk everywhere. It wasn't long after the war that she died, in the 1950s. She was fit, she just fell down the stairs, that's how she died. She was a couple of days laying there unconscious before she was found. But she would have lived to be 100, I reckon. Fit as a fiddle, and when you think of the abuse she took off her old man. My mum told us the story about him, my mum's dad. He disappeared and two years later he rolled up as though nothing had happened! They reckon he'd been to Canada working on the Southern Pacific Railway.

I remember dried eggs and powdered, that used to be made into scrambled eggs. The orange squash used to come in little flat bottles, very concentrated. Just a little drop of it would make a glass of orange. You got that if you had babies and there was always babies in our house.

Our house used to be the magnet to the rest of the kids because my mum was so easy-going.

My mum used to make lovely toffee apples and every kid that came in had a toffee apple. I don't know how she made the toffee but she would pour it over, put them in a big tray. You didn't have fridges, they just used to stand there and go hard.

We used to get berries at Beckenham Place Park. You could get blackberries, gooseberries, everything up there and bluebells. I love a bluebell because that always takes me back to Beckenham Place Park when I was a kid. The woods used to be all blue. I thought that was a beautiful sight. Everything running wild plus all the old apple trees down there in the gardens where people had abandoned their houses. We'd come home with the fruit. Nobody bothered, it was a freedom really, there was nobody to check you but then you didn't cause no problem. You didn't smash up the tree, you just took a few apples or pears or whatever. There was no vandalism.

**Chores**

In the winter me and my sisters, our job on a Saturday morning was to come down Southend Lane to the gasworks to get two hundredweight of coke. When you got down there the queue might be right outside the gate, so the whole Saturday morning was taken up getting your coke. That had to last you. A coalman used to come round but that was too expensive.

We had to carry it on a pram. Some of the kids whose dads weren't in the army had barrows which was nice but we always had a pram. Nine times out of ten the wheel would fall off. Southend Lane was a steep hill and there would be two or three kids of six or seven years old trying to push a pram with two hundredweight of coke. Oh, it was a horrible job! When we got home my mum would have been shopping down Deptford and we might have pie and mash from Manze's or we'd have nice thick bread and butter and it always seemed worth it.

Mum always did the jobs in the house. Dad never done nothing. If he done it, he done it half-heartedly and buggered it all up anyway. He was a bodger. Mum done the decorating, the repairing of shoes; anything that had to be done Mum done it. I can remember her decorating during the war, putting whitewash on the wall and then getting a sponge and putting different colours on. Now it's the trendy thing, but she was doing that 50 years ago when Dad wasn't there.

We all did bits and pieces at home. Obviously my sisters helped with the housework and ironing and they could all cook, but Mum done the majority of things. She was pretty good at everything. Mr Harris who lived just round the corner used to say my mum could mend shoes better than he could, better than any man in the street. I can remember her sitting up after we'd all gone to bed with the little lance repairing shoes. The times I see her fingers and thumbs cut where the knife had gone through when she's cutting the leather. She used to put studs in the bottom so they'd last forever, but they were good for sliding on. Even when my dad come out the army my mum still used to mend the shoes.

The rag-and-bone man used to come round and he'd give you goldfish for your rags. He'd weigh it up. Wool would probably be the best but we couldn't give that. If there was anything wool my mum would unpick it and re-knit it. With five daughters, by the time the clothes went from Rosie down to Thelma, even the rag man wouldn't take it!

## Cinema

In the winter your Saturday morning was taken up getting coke but the rest of the time I used to go to Saturday morning pictures if my mum could afford it. I mean if she gives it to the one she's got to give it to us all, so it might cost a shilling or more to get us our fares, although we used to walk most places. We very rarely caught a bus, only if we were going over our Nan's at Deptford which we used to do quite a lot. Even getting in the pictures it would be a penny or tuppence, so it would probably cost us sixpence or sevenpence all together. We used to go if she had bob to spare but we didn't press her.

The main films I remember were the old Tom Mix cowboys. It come to an end where an Indian would be firing at Tom Mix and you see the arrow going right through his back, and they'd say "Come back next week! Does he get killed or doesn't he get killed?" That gets you back. It's like a serial, like Coronation Street. You had to go next week to see whether he got killed, but you couldn't always do it. Obviously you used to bunk in if you could. But there wasn't a lot of that on Saturday morning pictures because it was all kids so they knew what was happening.

Our mum couldn't afford it so it was how many jam jars you managed to get during the week. You'd go down there and if one or two managed to get in, they'd push the bar of the exit and get a couple more in. Although there wasn't many park-keepers or police, there always seemed to be a lot of usherettes about at the time. We got caught a lot.

## Outings

Greenwich Pier, that was our seaside. Never can remember my dad with us, obviously most of it was during the war. "We'll go to the seaside today", but not only us. My mum used to take half the street with her as well. We would go down Greenwich Pier and they used to put sand on it and that was our seaside. We'd take sandwiches and a few sweets. It used to be packed with kids, just like sitting on the beach.

Mum used to take us over Blackheath Fair. My dad wouldn't do anything like that. He took us over there once and made us walk nearly all the way home from Blackheath to Bellingham, which is probably three or four miles. He didn't have the patience to wait for a bus. We were all carrying kids and walking along. They were crying and my dad was walking miles in front of us. He kept turning round: "Shut your moaning, we'll be home in a minute." He wouldn't wait for buses, we just walked nearly all the way home. We were all aged from two upwards.

He never took us out again. He wouldn't take us anywhere. I think my mum enjoyed herself more when he wasn't there. He was awful at kids. That's probably why we grew up that way, loving Mum, because she was dead opposite to the old man. She was always there.

## Home life

It was crazy in those days, there was noise all the time. As a kid all I can remember is lots of people and lots of noise. In my house there was seven kids so something was always going on, no matter what time of the day. My mum was always indoors. If you went to school and you got fed up or felt ill, you'd go home and your mum was there. She'd already done the shopping. How she managed to get everything done I don't know.

## Pawnshop

Everybody was poor, so if you did have anything like a decent set of clothes or a suit that would have to be pawned. Where we moved to there wasn't really a pawn shop so on a Monday my mum used to do up her little parcel and she'd say "I'm going to see Nan at Deptford". We didn't know. So she used to go to Deptford on a Monday with her little parcel, come home with food and then Saturday she'd go back to Depftord, see her mum again and come home with this little parcel. It would be sheets and pillow slips or Dad's suit, anything. We didn't have jewellery or things like that, we weren't that rich. I can remember she had a fox fur that went round her neck, that used to go in and out quite regular. Harvey & Thompson's down the High Street. We only found out about it when we grew up. She would go and get the Sunday clothes on Saturday because although we were like that we were made to go to church on a Sunday.

We always went to church Sunday morning. My mum made sure we went. Didn't do us no good obviously, but we went! She wasn't a religious person but she wouldn't do nothing wrong. If someone knocked on the door and you went "Oh Mum, tell them I'm not in", she'd say "I'm not going to lie for you". She'd swear and lie for a way to get you out of trouble or if it was for good, but not a little lie or lies that there was no need for. She believed you should be brought up right, although in circumstances such as with the lead there was nothing much she could do. It was there, so – I was a naughty boy because I could have killed myself; but that three pounds we made probably kept us going for three or four weeks during the war.

**We didn't have anything but we did have a laugh and we still do.**

All the money we made used to go to our mum. It was never for your own good. Maybe we kept a little bit for pictures or she give us some back for everything we brought home. She was there on her own but she always managed to get us the apple and orange at Christmas. Everything we had at Christmas was second-hand. I remember getting a bagatelle, a pinball game. It was second-hand and it was knocked about a bit but to me it was as though someone gave me a million pounds with all the little pins in it and the balls. She used to sit up all Christmas Eve, repairing or altering clothes for me or the girls. Washing and ironing all through Christmas and still be happy as a sandboy and still stay awake. She was always awake my mum, never asleep.

It was only when I got bigger that I realised we used to sit down for food and we'd all be eating. My sister would say "Why aren't you having something to eat, Mum?" She'd go "I'm not hungry, you eat yours, I'm not hungry." My mum was never hungry. We didn't realise, poor old cow, she was hungry all right but she gave the food to us. It's sad. As we got older we realised that of course she was hungry but she was giving the food to us. That was her favourite phrase: "No, I'm not hungry, no." "Have some of this, Mum." "No, don't want it, you eat it, I'm alright." That's how she was, she really was a diamond and always there, never out, never missing.

My mum never went abroad. I don't think she ever went up to the West End. She went to the seaside probably when she was getting old, but the furthest she ever went basically was hopping, just 20 or 30 miles from home.

She was friends with all the neighbours but she never went out with them. If she went out, she went out with Dad but never on her own. He wouldn't allow that. My dad was a very jealous person.

## Dad

I didn't really know what Dad was doing out there in Belgium, but I knew he was on the fiddle. We used to get letters now and again with coins in, half-a-crown or something like that. When he came home he had quite a lot of money. He got to know some rich Belgian people out there, a Colonel I think and they came over after the war.

He was quite a lad, the old man, but he used to send home a few bob now and again, not what he was earning. I think he was earning a fortune, one way or another. When he did come home on leave I can only remember him drunk, that used to be his thing.

He did care about us but he was a hard man. He wasn't a nice dad really. He was a hard, selfish man but he wouldn't see anybody hurt. Once after the war when a teacher was picking on my sister Sylvia my old man took the day off and come in the classroon.
"That him, Sylve?"
"Yeah", and he knocked the teacher all round the room, with all the kids cheering: "Go on, Mr White."
Another time was when this lad of about 20 was doing what they call a Chinese burn on my legs. I've still got the scars. One of my sisters went and got Dad and he come up. My dad was quite a big man.
"Which one was it?",
"It was him, Dad."

He went 'bang' and the bloke was flat out. He'd fight anybody, wasn't scared of anyone. He said, living in Blackhorse Road, you had to be like that.

He wanted all boys, that's why he had so many children. I'm not like him at all, though when I was a kid you had to be hard.

## Learning to be hard

My first job was at Penfold Motors, Lee Green. The son that married Diane Penfold was a friend of ours in Bellingham and he got me the job. I got the sack for clouting the foreman. He picked on me and I hit him, put him down in one punch and got the sack. But you had to, it was the way it was.

As a little child I was quite timid. We used to fight amongst each other, but I wasn't that hard. It was as I got older and bigger and started knowing that you had to fight your corner that I changed.

As for ducking and diving, you always done that. You had to to get by with a big family and the boys were the ones to do it. My Billy done his share. You didn't know you were doing it. You just went out and done it and you didn't realise you were doing wrong. I mean with that lead, I knew it was wrong but not seriously wrong. I knew that metal was worth money because you'd seen them coming round for it and I could have only been about seven. The way I looked at it, it was an empty house. Nobody owned it, nobody lived there, and there was stuff there that I knew was worth something. Once we got in the street and they said "You could get put away", that's when I knew.

My dad never clouted me. He clouted Billy, my brother. He got lots of clouts when he was little. Dad's brother, my Uncle Len, was a lovely man and he used to give Bill sixpence. Well, he gave us sixpence and it was just by Guy Fawkes night so Billy's going up the road and my dad was coming from the pub.
"Where are you going?"
"Going to buy some fireworks."
"Fireworks, where did you get the money?" He clouted my brother and he took the money off him as well.

Everybody liked my dad, they

thought he was lovely, but indoors he was a different man. Indoors he just looked at you and you'd stop what you were doing and that was hard when you were seven kids.

I think that was how he was brought up. He had a hard mother and father. He started work in a delicatessen when he was 12 years of age, with no shoes. He had to steal things. If he went home without a little bit of marge or butter or bacon, his mother would give him a clout for not taking something. They used to send his sister Violet up to the shop so he could give her stuff to take home. But then when he did get caught once he got clouted by the man that owned the shop who dragged him home and then he got clouted again when he got indoors for getting caught. So he didn't know any different. When he got old, he got milder and he thought we were all lovely, but it was a bit late. Although we didn't resent him or nothing. Dad bought me a meccano set and a little car. I was the only one he ever bought a toy for. I got on well with him because I was probably more like him than any of the others. I used to like my drink, so I was a bit like him, bit selfish maybe. He could drink 20 pints without much problem. He only used to drink the old dark ale.

He'd get his wages and he'd take out what he wanted for his beer and his bets and what was left over my mum would get. But he did provide all his life. He was never out of work. During the Depression, he was always ducking and diving and betting. They did send him away to a place called Belmont. If you were unemployed then you got sent away from home. They taught him tailoring and he was quite good with the needle for the sort of man he was. He could alter suits and things like that, quite handy.

He was away for five or six years during the war, and it was terrible when he came back. We never had a radio during the war so we used to sing. It sounds silly now, but we used to sit round singing, laughing and joking. My mum used to sing all the old songs, 'Don't go down in the mine, dad', and all things like that. If my sisters hear it now, they cry their eyes out. When Dad came home all that had to stop. He didn't like to see us happy, I suppose. Kids used to come and stay the night during the war. We never went anywhere else, all the other kids would stay with us. But when he came home he didn't want mates in and things like that.

The day before my 18th birthday I got nicked for being on the boats at Peter Pan's pool when it was closed. They had me in the cells. They come round to ours and got my dad out about two o'clock in the morning. They said "We got your son down the station. Will you come and get him?" but he went "Effing keep him down there, teach him a lesson". He was that sort of man. My sisters were crying so my brother Bill had to come and get me. They knocked on my door a few times afterwards and he used to go out and argue with them. He never got in any serious trouble but he'd say "F off. You done him once, now leave him alone" so he did stick up for you, if he thought you was all right.

He had a funny attitude, but if you met him, you'd love him. Always stand his corner. In the pub he'd have to get that first beer and if you were slow, he'd go up and get them again. He used to buy himself two pints of beer and while he was ordering the rest one would be gone. The drunker he got, the better he got at darts. He was a fantastic darts player. He used to throw from nine foot.

Just after he come home my dad had a habit of sitting on the best side, by the the fire, with his feet up on the mantlepiece. That was his usual position. After the war they used to turn the electric off or the gas, due to the shortages. Well, one Saturday morning my brother came home from work and there was no electric, no gas, so my mum was cooking him some food on the range and I was sitting in front of the fire. Anyway Mum said to Dad "Bill, watch your feet, there's a frying pan on the fire". Next minute he brought his foot down, the frying pan come over and all the fat went down my legs, smothered me. I screamed obviously and he went and got a pound of butter and put it all over it. The worst thing! My legs came out in massive big blisters, and do you know who he blamed? My brother got the blame for that, because it was his dinner that was being cooked. Through that I was in bed for about six months and I had to learn to walk again.

## VE Day

We had a party right the way along Overdown Road. It seemed the tables stretched for a mile. There must have been 50 children or more, plus all the women. Everybody supplied something, a table or chair, and food, and it wasn't "That's for my boy Johnny". Everybody supplied and everybody ate what they wanted. At that time there was quite a lot of parties because round our streets there was nice people. When the men came home from the war, it was "Mr So-and-so's coming home", so they'd give a little party. We lived on the crossroads and they had a fire there at every party. It would make a big dent in the tarmac and the council used to come round every time to repair it. All the houses had wooden gates and the bigger boys would go and get them and say "Number 26 Elfreda Crescent is going on now", and those who lived there would go "That's mine, don't", but it went on all the same, and there were never no fights.

But, yes, VE day was beautiful. 'There'll be bluebirds over the white cliffs of Dover' and all that. There was always a piano. Along our street there was Georgie Grant's sister. She only had one leg but she could play the piano-accordian. Everybody was singing and dancing. It was beautiful.

---

**Although the war was hard I can honestly say I can't remember being upset as a kid.**

---

I can remember hearing the fire engines going along. You used to watch for the doodlebug and when that light went out, you knew it had passed you over. You could virtually name the road where it was going, so all the kids would run round there. You'd see the houses flattened and within no time the old fire engines would be coming round.

You know it's funny that I never knew anyone that got injured and not one of my cousins or uncles got killed in the war. Very, very fortunate for the size of the family.

## After the war

The atmosphere did change afterwards. Things started getting back to normal. Kids had to go to school, the husbands came back and I suppose there was a lot of tension at home. The way I feel, when there's just one parent at home, there's no tension. When you get two there's conflict. So there came a lot of tension and I think people started wanting whereas during the war nobody wanted anything. It wasn't there, you didn't have the money so you didn't crave. People now, they want too much, but then I suppose when the men come home from the war they'd done four, five, six years abroad, they wanted something. So they started bettering themselves and that put strains on people. When they come home the wages wasn't high enough. I mean probably my father wasn't earning enough to look after seven kids, which goes for a lot of the men. So there again there must be tension. Our joys were not over but certainly subdued when my father come home.

People carried on doing things together in the street for quite a long time after the war. The kids were still the same. Indoors it was different. Out in the street we were still the same. Still had fun, although my father wouldn't let us have bikes, or anything movable, scooters, skates. Too dangerous. He wouldn't allow us to go swimming. Though he didn't do nothing for us, he wouldn't let us do dangerous things so he must have loved us dearly. Anything we did we had to sneak and hide and do when he wasn't there.